TRADITIONAL NEEDLE ARTS

QUILTING

TRADITIONAL NEEDLE ARTS

QUILTING

Over 20 classic step-by-step projects

DIANA LODGE

PHOTOGRAPHY BY DAVID MONTGOMERY

THUNDER BAY
P·R·E·S·S

To Roy, who has unstintingly (and patiently) given artistic and moral help and support at every stage of this book

Published by Thunder Bay Press
5880 Oberlin Drive, Suite 400
San Diego, California 92121

First published in Great Britain in 1995
by Mitchell Beazley, an imprint of Reed Consumer Books Limited
Michelin House, 81 Fulham Road, London SW3 6RB
and Auckland, Melbourne, Singapore and Toronto

Art Director	JACQUI SMALL
Executive Editor	JUDITH MORE
Executive Art Editor	LARRAINE SHAMWANA
Editors	JULIA NORTH &
	HEATHER DEWHURST
Designer	BEN BARRETT
Production Controller	MICHELLE THOMAS
Photographer	DAVID MONTGOMERY
Stylist	KATRIN CARGILL
Illustrators	KUO KANG CHEN &
	MICHAEL HILL

Library of Congress Cataloging-in-Publication data

Lodge, Diana.
Quilting: more than 20 classic projects/Diana Lodge;
photography by David Montgomery.
p. cm -- (Traditional needle arts)
Includes index.
ISBN 1-57145-062-9
1. Quilting--Patterns. 2. Quilts. I. Title II. Series.
TT835.L623   1995   95-23305
746.46'041--cc20   CIP

Typeset in Perpetua 12/16 and 10/12pt
Printed and bound in Barcelona, Spain
by Cayfosa

Contents

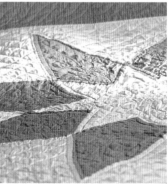

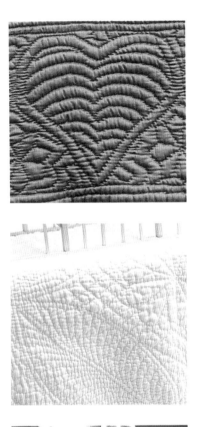

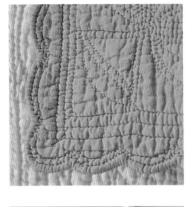

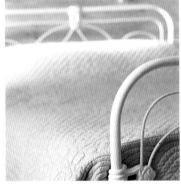

Introduction

Quilting is a needle art, essentially a form of embroidery, with an addictive subtlety all its own. As the light falls on a beautifully designed and exquisitely executed antique quilt, the densely stitched areas are contrasted with the more open areas where larger motifs stand out in relief, and there is a delightful harmony between the tactile nature of the fabric and the graphic qualities of the quilting design.

Although the word "quilt" can apply to any covering in which two fabrics are stitched together – with or without a warm middle layer – including patchwork and appliqué covers, in this book the emphasis is on the quilting stitches and designs. Some of the quilt tops are pieced, but their beauty lies chiefly in their quilting patterns.

The word quilt is derived from the Latin *culcita* – a stuffed sack, mattress, or pillow. But, although the notion of stitching several layers of fabric together for warmth and decoration predates even the Romans by many centuries, and quilted armor existed in the days of William the Conqueror, quilting as it is found in this book had its origins in the "*cowltes*" or "*qwhiltez*" of medieval Europe, or even later, in the beautifully quilted doublets, breeches, and petticoats that were high fashion throughout Europe in the 17th century.

Early quilts and quilted clothing appear to have been almost exclusively for the rich. That ill-fated child Catherine Howard received 23 quilts out of the Royal Wardrobe before her marriage to Henry VIII (rather like the story of the princess and the pea, but without the happy ending). The fabrics were silks and satins, and much of the quilting was flat, with no middle layer; it was often decorated

LEFT This distinctive red and white star design is an excellent example of a Durham quilt. The stitching on the piece helps to emphasize the pattern. Quilting thrived in the north of England during the 19th century.

ABOVE Detail of a "strippy" quilt; a good beginners' project.
BELOW Amish quilts are characterized by bold colors and lovely quilting.

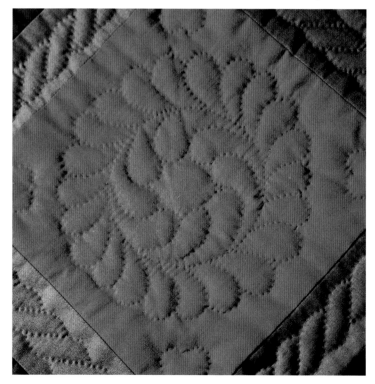

with embroidery. Bed hangings and covers were expensive showpieces – they were essentially a statement about the owner's wealth and importance. The poor of the early 16th century, in stark contrast, often lacked even a sheet to protect them from their straw bedding. Even by the end of the following century, quilted covers remained solely a rich man's luxury.

However, in the 18th century, this began to change. The fashion for elaborate quilted petticoats extended throughout society, and poorer women learned to make their own copies, continuing long after quilted clothing had ceased to be fashionable among the middle and upper classes. At the same time, even the humblest of homes were becoming steadily more prosperous. By the late 18th century, bedcoverings in small farms and cottages may well have included woolen or linsey-wolsey (linen/wool) quilts. Imported cottons became increasingly plentiful, to be superseded – as the Industrial Revolution got underway – by home-produced cottons, and this was eventually to become the most popular fabric of all for quilts.

By the 19th century, quilts had become the standard bedcovering in rural communities, both in Britain and in the United States. Pure quilting formed part of the needlework tradition of the early American settlers; the American Museum in Bath, England, contains a magnificent blue calamanco (glazed worsted) wholecloth quilt made in the middle of the 18th century. However, by the second half of the 19th century, most American quilt tops were of patchwork or appliqué, with the quilting generally only echoing the dominant fabric pattern. Only among the Amish communities in America, where complex patchwork and appliqué were deemed frivolous for religious reasons, did quilting not only survive, but actually flourish.

Amish quilters restricted their pieced work to a minimum, and today these wonderful quilts, with their strong, dark, yet vibrant color contrasts and beautiful quilting, are among the most highly prized of all American antique quilts. Also at this time, French quilters were making quilts ranging from the highly elaborate – exemplified by the wedding quilts known as *courtepointes,* and the decorative yellow quilt which can be seen on page 104 – to those designed primarily for warmth. *Courtepointes* were

usually made by the bride's mother using a scarf that is printed on only three sides; on the fourth side, a matching strip of printed fabric was added.

In Britain throughout most of the 19th century, quilting was widespread, and regional differences began to emerge. In the West Country, quilts were generally filled with carded fleece, and designs were particularly free-flowing and naturalistic.

Writing in the 1930s, the quilting historian Elizabeth Hake was only able to contact three West Country women who had been quilters within the previous sixty years, but one of them recalled how her mother and grandmother would pick sprays of oak, ivy, clover, and thistles to draw their quilting patterns from life – combining oak with ivy, "as they grow together." It is particularly interesting to note that many of the early American settlers came from the west of England, and the American wholecloth quilt mentioned earlier features a similarly naturalistic flowing design.

Welsh quilts, on the other hand, tended to be more geometric in character, with patterns contained within clearly defined series of borders. They were generally filled either with wool or even with old blankets and cast-off clothing, and many are therefore relatively heavy.

ABOVE The quilt shown here is a wholecloth quilt from the north of England. The central motif has a large feathered circle with a rose in the center and large leaves around the inside.

In the north of England, quilting thrived in the 19th century – particularly in the North Pennine dales of Teesdale, Allendale, and Weardale, and also in the nearby mining areas around Durham. The women here prided themselves on their quilting skills, and 19th-century North Country quilts remain sought-after collectors' items. In contrast to the Welsh quilts, these were filled with a thin batting of cotton, with a cotton top and backing. The humble, everyday quilts were the pieced "strippies" (examples of which can be seen on pages 34, 45, and 50), but pride of place went to the wholecloth quilts. These had elaborate borders and centers, generally less geometric in design than the Welsh quilts, but with floral and other motifs that were more stylized and abstract than those of the West Country quilts.

Both in Wales and in the North Country, quilting was one of the fundamental skills of every competent housewife, but there were also professional quilters – these included village quilters, the itinerant quilters of Wales who would travel from farmhouse to farmhouse helping to make the next year's supply of quilts, the "stampers" of Northern England who designed and marked quilt tops for a living, and the women who ran the quilt clubs in mining communities in both areas. One of the most influential stampers was George Gardiner, who ran a shop in Dorespool, in Allendale, and began to mark quilt tops around the middle of the 19th century. Little is known about him, but it seems to have been he who developed the style of open, flowing borders and centers, with a minimum of demarcation lines, for which quilts in this area became famous. Elizabeth Sanderson (see page 77 for the pink & white star project) was his most famous apprentice.

Quilting started to decline in popularity – even in Wales and northern England – around the turn of the century, but the tradition was

ABOVE Heavily sculptured leaf designs were particularly popular on Welsh quilts. The designs are often quite geometric as opposed to free-flowing.

kept alive by club quilters. Little or no welfare was available in those days, and a woman who found herself the breadwinner, perhaps after her husband had been injured or even killed in a mining accident, might found a quilt club. A group of customers would each contribute a small weekly sum, and each in turn would eventually receive a finished quilt. To some extent, these clubs survived up to and even after World War I, not so much because the quilts were needed (indeed, they were becoming rather unfashionable), but because they helped families to survive with dignity.

In the late 1920s and 1930s, there was a government-backed effort, under the British Rural Industries Bureau, to revive quilting as a home industry. Under the scheme, which flourished until the outbreak of World War II in 1939, quilters in both Wales and County Durham produced luxury wholecloth quilts for the London market. After the war, quilting almost died out as a living craft in Britain, being kept alive by only a small handful of women, including Amy Emms (see page 66, for the feather wreath pillows project). This is until recently, however, when in Europe and America we have once again come to appreciate the beauty and artistry of antique quilts.

A wide range of quilts and patterns is shown in this book. Although many traditional patterns were used time and time again, there is ample scope for variation and individuality. Welsh quilters, in particular, prided themselves on never repeating a design exactly, so allow yourself the freedom to adapt these designs, introducing your own individual motifs and patterns, to make treasured heirlooms for the future.

ABOVE A fine star quilt, possibly marked by Elizabeth Sanderson.
BELOW A highly decorative French wholecloth quilt.

Before You Begin

The quilt projects in this book vary greatly in terms of the skill and time required to make them. An indication of the degree of skill required is given with each of the projects, but this is a rough guide; a skilled dressmaker or embroiderer will obviously find the projects much simpler than someone with little sewing experience. Success with one of the large-scale wholecloth quilts included in this book is achieved by determination and a methodical

nature, rather than advanced sewing skills. So if you have experimented enough to decide that you enjoy quilting and have fallen for one of the more complex designs, don't be daunted!

MATERIALS AND EQUIPMENT
Fabrics
In the past, quilters used a variety of fabrics for the fronts and backs of their quilts, including fine wool, silk, and linen, but as can be seen from this book, the majority of antique quilts that survive today are made from pure dressweight cotton (see left). This is easy to sew, hardwearing, and remains an ideal fabric, particularly for anyone new to quilting. It is possible to quilt with cotton/polyester mixtures but on the whole, synthetic fibers are neither as durable nor as easy to sew, and are best avoided.

Fabrics with a slight sheen can show up quilting patterns to advantage, as the light reflects off the raised areas. In addition to silks, polished cottons and cotton sateen have sometimes been used. The former, however, has the disadvantage that the glaze can wear away with repeated washing.

A problem familiar to quilters is "bearding," where fibers from the filling work their way through to the surface. To avoid this, choose closely woven fabrics, whatever the fiber. A cotton fabric with around 68–78 threads per inch is ideal; cotton sheeting, which often has a high thread count, may prove too closely woven for ease of stitching.

Woolen fabrics, in particular, can be spoiled by bearding, the trouble being that very closely woven woolen fabrics can be heavy and difficult to sew, whereas the lighter woolens may be too loosely woven. A good-quality batting will help to minimize difficulties.

If you are experimenting with a silk fabric, choose a good-quality, firmly woven silk, such as a Shanghai silk.

Remember that silks can easily be "weighted" by adding chemicals, so unless you are an expert, you will not always be able to tell the quality of a silk by feeling it; buy the best you can afford from a reputable supplier.

It is normal to use the same fabric, or the same type of fabric in a contrasting color or print, for the back as for the front. If you are piecing strips, use fabrics of the same weight and type, to avoid puckering at the seams.

It is not always necessary to wash fabrics before using them for quilting; indeed, a certain amount of shrinkage after washing can help to emphasize the quilting patterns. Again, if you have chosen a reasonably good-quality fabric, it should not shrink excessively. If you are joining fabrics of different colors — on a strippy, for example — you will wish to make sure that the fabrics are colorfast. To check this, soak any suspect fabric in a solution of three parts cold water to one part vinegar. Rinse thoroughly, and then wash again with a piece of white fabric. If the latter is discolored, discard the dubious fabric.

Batting
Most of the antique quilts in this book were made with a cotton filler, but quilters these days have the option of using synthetic battings. These are available in a choice of weights, the 2-ounce weight being generally the best for hand-quilting. Thicker types give more "loft" (the relief effect characteristic of quilting), but are harder to

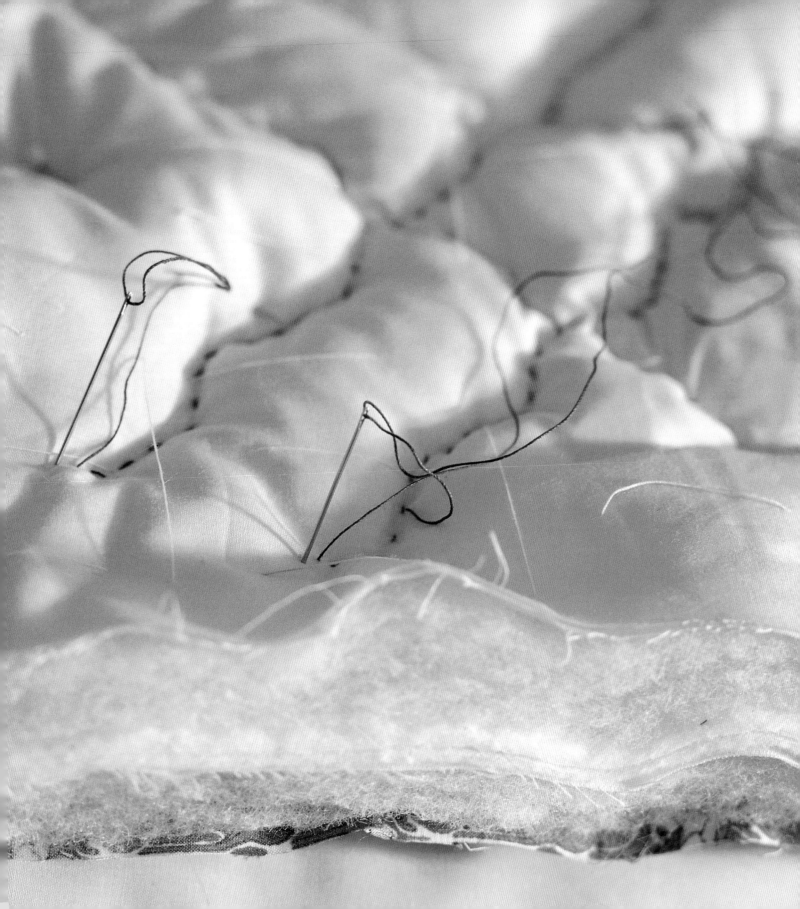

stitch through, and you will make fewer stitches per inch. To avoid bearding, buy good-quality bonded synthetic batting, which is finished with a heat-sealed bonding resin. (Some quilters find that the bonding makes stitching more difficult, so experiment with different types until you find one you like.) Specially prepared cotton battings are also available. These have less loft than polyester, but of course will produce a soft effect, closer to the originals in this book. Batting made from cotton mixed with 20 percent polyester is now also available, offering the best qualities of both. This batting should be preshrunk in hot water, as it tends to shrink with washing; soak and spin the batting. Wool battings are not always readily available and tend to suffer from bearding. A layer of cheesecloth or gauze between the wool and the quilt surface will help to overcome this problem.

NOTE: Unless otherwise stated, the fabric quantities listed with each project assume a standard fabric width of 45 inches. If your fabric is wider or narrower than this, you will have to estimate the length required; add at least 2 inches each way to the dimensions given for the finished quilt, and allow ½ inch for each seam allowance.

Threads

Ordinary dressmakers' threads are not strong enough for quilting. A variety of quilting threads are available, made from pure cotton, polyester, or mixtures of both. You may find that it helps to assist the thread to pass smoothly through the layers if you pull it through a beeswax block.

Marking equipment

The marker should be chosen to suit the particular color and type of fabric, the quilting method (hoop, which will require much handling of the fabric, or frame, which will not), and the washability of the finished article (whether the marked line can be sponged or washed away after quilting).

Pens and pencils Silver and soapstone pencils, available from quilting suppliers, leave marks that are almost invisible after quilting. Other quilters prefer to use a colored pencil in a shade just slightly darker than that of the fabric. White or cream fabrics can be marked with a lead pencil; do not mark with an ordinary pencil – use a propelling pencil that can take a fine ⅟₅₀-inch H lead.

Chalk Chalk-based markers, such as dressmakers' pencils, have the advantage and disadvantage of being easily removable; if you are using a hoop or tube frame, the constant handling will wear away chalk lines quickly.

Masking tape This can be placed lightly on fabric as a guideline for straight filler-pattern lines.

Carpenter's square Use a set square for checking.

Flexible curve This is very useful for marking repeated curving lines.

Rulers A quilter's ruler, which is a large, wide plastic ruler marked with angles and a grid, is a very useful tool. A long rule and a rolling ruler are also useful for marking filling patterns.

Templates See page 19.

Sewing equipment

The major investment here is a hoop or frame to hold the layers in place as you quilt. It is essential to have one the other, as both hands are needed for quilting.

Hoops and tube frames Quilting hoops are large wooden hoops, sometimes free-standing; the fabric layers are held between inner and outer rings. Small tube frames, again in free-standing or lap-held versions, are available, with the fabric layers held in plastic grips. Both these types are less expensive and take up less space than a full-scale frame, but the work must be removed from the hoop or frame between sessions, and the layers must be thoroughly basted together.

Quilt frames A large wooden quilting frame is the traditional method of holding the fabric layers during quilting. It consists of two bars, long enough to carry the full width of the quilt, spaced apart by two stretchers, exposing an area deep enough for comfortable working. The frame can rest on trestles or a table top, or there are free-standing, pivoting versions. One disadvantage is cost (unless you know someone who can make one for you), another problem the space required. The advantages are that the layers do not need to be basted; the work remains in the frame until finished, and a much larger area is exposed for working.

Other equipment

Needles Use "between" needles; most beginners start with a size 8, but the shorter, finer 10–12 sizes are better for fine work.

Pins Use long, fine pins – the ones with glass or plastic heads are ideal.

Thimbles Quilting is hard on the fingers, so it is usual to wear a thimble on the middle finger of the (top) quilting hand when hand-quilting, and you may also find it helpful to wear one on your thumb. The middle finger of the underneath hand, which returns the needle to the surface,

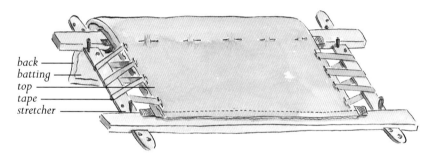

back
batting
top
tape
stretcher

ABOVE Quilting frame

is also vulnerable. A large selection of leather, plastic, and metal thimbles and finger protectors have now been developed, and even if you have always hated using a thimble, it is worth giving these a try until you find a type that suits you.

Scissors Good-quality dressmakers' scissors are an essential tool; smaller embroidery scissors are useful for cutting thread ends.

MARKING THE FABRIC
Marking your design
Some quilters in the past used to mark center and main border lines, then finish marking the quilt when it was in the frame, but unless you are very experienced, it is best to mark your design on the quilt top before assembling the layers (top, batting, and backing) together.

Very thoroughly and carefully steam press the top and lay it, right side up, on a large table. Use drafting tape or tablecloth clips to anchor the fabric to the table and keep it taut. Keep your marking tools and templates on a side table, and make sure that you have access to all sides of the large table. Mark the outer edge of the quilting design with either a single or double line, bearing in mind the way in which the quilt edges will be finished; if the edges are to be folded in the quilting should, 1 inch clear of

the raw edge, and in other cases it should stop about ½ inch clear. Also draw other important design divisions, such as border lines, and lines dividing the quilt into quarters. If these lines will not be quilted, but are only guidelines, use basting thread or an easily removable marker.

Next, draw the central design, then other motifs and border patterns. Start at the middle of each border and work out to the corners, to ensure that the pattern is symmetrical. If you are using a template to draw a repeated border design or filling pattern, such as a twist border, use the registration notches on the template to make sure that the repeats are accurate. Take care when drawing around a template to follow the edge exactly with your pencil/marker. Finally, draw any filling patterns, such as parallel lines. Check regularly with a ruler and square or protractor as you are drawing filling patterns.

NOTE: If the filling is cotton, as is the case with most of the old quilts in this book, the distance between quilting lines should not be larger than 2 inches, but with modern synthetic batting, increase this to 3 inches.

ASSEMBLING THE LAYERS
Using a hoop or tube frame
Once you have marked the quilt top, the next stage is to assemble the three

layers – top, batting and back – together. If you are using a hoop or tube frame, mark the mid-point on each edge of each of the layers with pins, then carefully smooth out the well-pressed quilt back, wrong side up, on a large flat surface. Fold the batting in half and lay it on the back, matching marked mid-points. Gently unfold the batting over the second half of the back, again checking that pinned mid-points match. Fold the top into quarters, right side inside, and carefully place it over one quarter of the two prepared layers. Gradually unfold, matching up mid-points, and smoothing out wrinkles with a long ruler or yardstick.

Pin the layers together, and then baste very thoroughly with horizontal and vertical lines not more than 4–6 inches apart and with diagonals from corner to corner. For basting lines running across the quilt, start at the center, leaving a long thread end and working out to one edge; rethread the needle at the center of the quilt and work out to the opposite edge. In this way, you will avoid a cluster of knots at the center.

Center the quilt over the inner hoop, carefully smoothing out the fabric; loosen the outer hoop and place it over the quilt and the inner hoop. Tighten the outer hoop, making sure that the layers are smooth at the back as well as the front and are evenly stretched. Start quilting at the center, radiating outward, and always remove the quilt after each stitching session, to avoid marking the fabric.

Using a frame
Don't baste the layers together, but baste the backing fabric, wrong side up, to the webbing of the front and back rails and roll it up until flat;

smooth the batting and then the top fabric over it, pinning and basting these layers to the nearer rail. At the farther rail, pin the layers together and fold the excess batting and top fabrics.

Use tape 1 inch wide to tension the side edges, but leave enough flexibility for stitching. At each side, the tape is pinned to all three layers, then taken over the side stretcher, back up to the quilt layers, and pinned again, until both sides are pinned.

When quilting, work across the top to the far rail; roll the completed section onto the near rail, and re-pin and re-tape before continuing.

QUILTING

Take a 18-inch length of quilting thread, in the same color as the fabric to be quilted; thread it through a "between" needle, and knot the end. Insert the needle through the top and batting, about ¾ inch from the start of the quilting line; bring the needle out at the line, and pull the knot through the top, losing it in the batting.

Quilt with running stitches, using the index finger of the hand below the quilt to push the needle back up to the surface, and wearing a thimble on the middle finger of your top (sewing) hand to push it back and your thumb to press down the fabric ahead of the stitches. With practice, you will be able to take several stitches at a time, rocking the needle up and down with your thimbled finger before pulling the thread through. The number of stitches that you take will vary according to the type and thickness of your filling, and your experience, but the important thing is to maintain a rhythm of even, neat stitches. Assuming that you are using a 2-ounce

batting, aim for about six stitches per 1 inch to begin with. If you have reached the end of a pattern line and still have thread to continue, take the needle through the filling to the next line. If this is more than a needle-length away, you can "travel" by bringing the needle eye up through the top, swiveling the needle around, and continuing toward the next pattern line.

When you are quilting motifs, follow the natural flow of a curve, a flower petal for example, rather than quilting the entire motif outline first and then the inner details.

To finish at the end of a pattern line, make a small knot close to the last stitch; make a small stitch and pull the thread through to the back, anchoring the knot in the filling. If you are partway along a line, make a backstitch and run the thread through the batting, following along the unstitched line and taking a few tiny stitches, about ¼ inch apart; run the thread back through the filling and trim. The tiny stitches will be secured when you continue with the quilting.

In many cases, you will find it is best to use several needles, each for an individual pattern line – for example, when working the parallel lines of a filler pattern.

STITCHES
Feather stitch

A looped stitch, like chain stitch, that has "branched" stitches alternating on each side of the central line.

Backstitch

This consists of short, even stitches forming a continuous line on the surface and double-length stitches underneath. Bring needle a short way along stitching line; reinsert it at the start of the line, then bring it up beyond the first exit point, continuing in this way.

Herringbone stitch

On the lower line, bring the needle out at the left-hand side and insert on the upper line to the right, taking a stitch to the left with thread below needle. Insert needle on lower line to the right, and take a stitch to the left with the thread above the needle.

Slipstitch

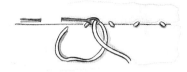

This is a nearly invisible stitch formed by slipping the thread under a fold of fabric. It can be used to join two folded edges, or one folded edge to a flat surface. Slide needle through the folded edge and, at the same place, pick up the thread of the under-fabric. Continue, spacing stitches ⅛–¼ inches apart.

Chain stitch

This is worked on two parallel lines. Bring the needle out at top left. Hold the thread down with the needle at top right. Bring the needle out again at bottom left, leaving the loop formed slightly loose. Insert the needle bottom right and bring it out over the looped thread in position for the next stitch.

FINISHING THE EDGES
Folded edges
First take a line of quilting around the edge – the finished quilt will extend ½ inch from this line, and the unfinished edges must extend at least 1 inch beyond the quilting. The batting is then trimmed to within ¼ inch of the line, and the cover fabrics to 1 inch.

First take the backing evenly over the batting; work around the quilt, one edge at a time, pinning as you go. Fold in the front, aligning it with the backing. Pin the two together, finishing with a double or single row of hand- or machine-stitching. In some cases, the folded edges of the quilts in this book have slightly different dimensions, in which case instructions are given with the project.

Self-binding
Including a ¼-inch seam allowance all around, allow sufficient backing fabric to create the required depth of border (in other words, if the border is to be 2 inches deep, the backing should extend 2¼ inches beyond the intended finished edge).

Finish all edges, trimming the top to a minimum of ½ inch from the

outer quilted line, and the batting to the finished edge of the border. Fold in the seam allowance around the backing, and bring the backing to the front, covering the edges of the batting and top. Start with the top and bottom edges of the quilt, and then fold over the sides, either mitering or making straight folds at the corners. Secure with hand running stitches or machine-stitching.

Separate binding
For this, you can either use one of the patchwork fabrics or a contrast fabric. Unless the edge is very curved, there is no need to cut the binding strip on the bias; it should be twice the finished depth of the bound edge, plus two seam allowances (½ inch).

Trim all layers to the finished size; the raw edges should be at least ½ inch from the outermost quilted line. Press the ¼-inch seam allowance down one long edge of the binding to the wrong side, and fold over one short edge by ½ inch. Start in the middle of one side edge of the quilt, matching raw edges and with right sides together (top of quilt and right side of binding), pin the binding to the quilt.

Machine-stitch the binding in position. Stitch up to the corner, decreasing the length of the stitches as you approach the corner; at the corner, raise the presser foot and, with the needle down through the fabric layers, pivot, making a 90° turn before continuing down the next edge. Leave an ample tuck in the binding at the corner, to enable you to bring the binding smoothly over to the back. Finally, overlap the folded short edge of binding with the raw short edge by about ½ inch. Bring the free, folded edge of the binding to the back of the quilt, just covering the

stitching line. At the corners, fold the fabric neatly for a mitered effect, and then slipstitch the binding to the back of the quilt, using matching thread.

TEMPLATES
Either make outline templates, filling in internal details by hand, or stencil templates, cutting the major internal lines with long dashes, just wide enough to allow your pencil lead to pass through. Filling in the lines freehand has its advantages: it is not difficult, and the effect can be more natural and attractive than stenciled lines. For templates, you will need either stiff cardboard or template plastic, spray adhesive, good scissors (preferably including a curved pair for tight corners and curves), craft knife and cutting mat. The templates shown in this book have been reduced in size and must be increased to the size stipulated. On modern photocopiers, it is possible to increase sizes accurately, for example from 3½ inches to 6 inches. Your local photocopy agency can do this for you.

Leaving about ¼ inch around each photocopied full-size shape, cut out the template patterns. Using spray adhesive, glue each shape either to firm cardboard or to template plastic. Leave to dry and then, using a craft knife or scissors, carefully cut out the shapes along the marked (outer) line. Using a craft knife and cutting mat, cut the dashes along the internal lines, if you wish to include these as guidelines. If you are using cardboard for your templates and a shape is repeated frequently, make several copies of the same shape, as cardboard templates can soon become worn.

Pieced & Simple Quilting

The quilts and quilted items in this section embrace a wide range of skills and include several suggestions for attractive practice pieces for those who are quilting for the first time, as well as some much more ambitious projects, such as the pink & white star quilt on page 77 or the Amish quilt on page 71. If you are new to quilting and would like to make a full-scale quilt, you might enjoy making a strippy, like those shown on pages 34, 45, and 50. You can also choose from a variety of templates to make your own individual quilt.

Lined Basket

This attractively shaped basket – lined with quilted fabric to protect the contents – can act as a portable needlework holdall. It could also be used for a variety of other storage purposes, including baby-changing equipment or toys. You will find that the quilted lining can totally transform a plain basket, and if you have a rustic style of basket, made with scratchy lengths of roughly cut twig or bark, the quilted lining will serve to protect the contents from damage.

Whatever size or shape of basket you choose, it is quite simple to make a pattern: either cut and fit paper (sheets of newspaper or lengths of brown paper should be large enough even for a much bigger basket than the one shown here), or use old sheets to make a pattern. It is not necessary to make the shaping too elaborate; the lining of the basket seen here is formed from three simple pieces – a circular base section, a circular lid cut to fit the top, and a long straight section. The latter was cut to the depth of the basket, plus the top hem and seam allowances, and to the (maximum) circumference of the basket, plus seam allowances.

As the top of this basket is wider than the base, the side section had to be roughly gathered into the base piece; if your basket narrows down consider-ably and you feel the gathering might be too bulky, stitch close to the edge of the seamline, about ⅛ inch into the quilted side, then trim the batting back to the stitched line before seaming the quilted sections together. To complete the top, the quilting was simply turned under and unobtrusively laced to the basket with quilting thread. To make the lid firm, it was formed from two quilted circles, with a cardboard layer between them, with the edge being finished with bias binding.

For the side piece, you could choose one of the strippy patterns on pages 34 or 50; for the lid and base, choose a circular design, such as a rose or feathered circle, or a scallop shape (see page 123).

If the basket is oblong in shape, you might adapt one of the "flat-iron" designs found on some of the strippies. These templates were originally made by placing two flat-irons (in the days when ironing entailed having a row of irons heating up in front of the fire) with their straight ends together, drawing around the joined shape, then filling the middle with flowers or other patterns. If your basket has a handle, you might like to adapt further this shape by using two separate pieces of cardboard for the inner stiffening, and leaving just fabric layers along the central line, to make a hinge.

RIGHT A perfect container for your knitting or needlework, or to hold quilting markers, threads, and needles, a basket such as this can easily be lined with quilted fabric. Formed from only three pieces of fabric – base, long straight section, and lid – this is a fairly simple project to undertake.

Placemats and Bread Basket

A set of placemats, accompanied by a long bread tray with a quilted lining to keep rolls warm, offers an ideal introduction to quilting. The placemats are approximately 15 inches in diameter and, as with the oven glove and holders on page 28, it might be a good idea to consider using a cotton batting if you are likely to use them to protect a table from very hot plates.

The basket has been lined in much the same way as the basket on page 22. However, because of its elongated shape, it uses four separate pieces – the sides have been formed from two long strips, with short end pieces. You might feel that the seams are too bulky for your particular basket. If this is the case, you could always use the quilt-as-you-go technique for joining seams (see page 36).

You will find several circular designs that would be suitable for the placemats throughout this book, including roses (pages 101 and 113), a feathered wreath (page 69) and a laurel wreath (page 107). Simply ask your local photocopy agency to expand the outline to the required size. As an alternative, you could use another traditional and very popular motif, the Lover's Knot (page 123), which is made from a quarter-knot template, repeated four times and linked. Traditional knot designs can be found in Celtic art books, which feature many intertwined shapes such as knots, crosses, and figurative animals, that convert well to quilting designs.

One way to make circular templates is to use a folded paper technique. Begin by drawing a circle on paper of a weight and type that is suitable for a pattern piece – tissue paper, for example. You could use also a pair of compasses, but if you are making placemats, it might be a simpler option to choose a large dinner plate.

Cut out the circle and then fold it in half, then in half again, then a third time, producing a wedge with eight thicknesses of paper. Take care to make the folds very crisp and accurate, so that each segment is identical. At the outer, curved edge of the wedge, where the thicknesses of paper are separate, draw a shaped edge; you might, for example, increase the shape of the curve by rounding it down at the corners. Cut along the marked shape, through all thicknesses, then unfold the paper. This will produce a basic rose outline, which you can complete with a variety of internal lines. Similarly, a "v" shape, with the point at the center of the curve of the wedge, will give you an eight-pointed star.

A set of quilted placemats offers an ideal opportunity to turn practice pieces into a lovely gift.

LEFT A set of quilted placemats, as shown here, offers an ideal opportunity to turn practice pieces into a lovely gift. Several of the circular designs found within the book – including roses, feathered wreaths, and laurel wreaths – would be suitable as the central design on a set of placemats.

Scented Hearts

Filled with potpourri, these heart-shaped sachets would make very charming, attractive gifts. The ones seen here were salvaged from a larger piece of quilting which was too worn in certain places for practical use. The quilting on these sachets, therefore, has a somewhat random appearance, although you might prefer to use a traditional heart motif.

Hearts were frequently, though not exclusively, found on bridal quilts, and the outline can be filled in many different ways. One example can be found on the Welsh quilt on page 87. Other hearts to be seen on antique quilts include heart shapes filled with smaller hearts of decreasing sizes (rather like a traditional Russian doll), hearts with two flowers growing from the base, and hearts filled with various forms of scroll design (see page 123).

If you are making your own paper pattern, you will want to achieve a balanced shape. The easiest way to do this is to fold a sheet of paper and draw one side of the heart only, making the foldline the central, vertical dividing line.

If you are using a hoop, you will probably find it easier – and more economical – to make a pair of hearts. Simply arrange four heart motifs (two back sections and two fronts) in a circular formation, with the points facing inward. Start by marking the outer fabric with the heart motif of your choice, making sure that you leave a space of at least two seam allowances between the marked outer lines of the motifs. Assemble the layers together (see page 17); set the fabric in a hoop or frame, then quilt the design.

When you have finished quilting, cut the motifs apart, leaving a ½-inch seam allowance around each. For additional security, stitch around the seamline of each shape, then put two hearts with right sides together, and again stitch around the seamline – leaving a small gap on one side for turning and filling. Trim the batting almost back to the seamline; then turn the heart right side out. Then fill your sachet with potpourri, and slipstitch the opening to close. To finish, stitch a ribbon hanging loop to the center. Repeat to make the second heart.

If you would like to intensify the perfumed fragrance, this can be achieved by rinsing the heart sachets in water scented with a potpourri refresher oil before you fill and seal the hearts.

This is a fairly simple project which will not take up too much of your time, but the results – as shown here – can be very effective.

RIGHT These heart sachets, filled with potpourri, can make lovely gifts. To enhance the fragrance, rinse the finished quilting in water scented with potpourri refresher oil before filling and sealing these perfumed hearts. The quilting pattern on these hearts is somewhat random, but you could use a traditional heart motif instead.

Oven Gloves

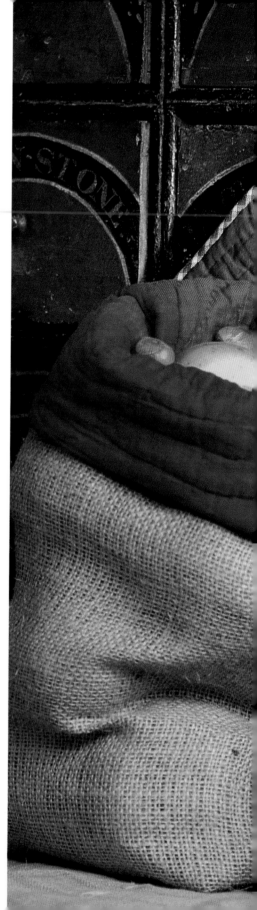

Small pieces of quilting can be put to many uses — oven gloves and potholders are a practical and traditional option. In general, most quilters these days prefer to use synthetic batting, which is easily washable and does not need to be so closely quilted as fillings made from natural fibers. However, it is well worth experimenting with wool and cotton — particularly in this case — as both are far less flammable than polyester, and they tend to char rather than burn.

In any event, if you are becoming a quilting enthusiast, you will want to experiment with these traditional fillings in order to appreciate the subtle differences in texture that they have to offer in comparison with synthetic battings. Although the latter have more "loft," with the fabric rising higher between the areas flattened by quilted lines, cotton and wool fillings give a gentler, more flowing quality. Wool tends to suffer from bearding — the fibers working out through the outer layers — but you can add a layer of fine cotton fabric between the batting and the outer fabric to avoid this.

To make the oven glove pattern, either copy an existing glove or draw loosely around your own hand and wrist. Make a pair of mirror-image quilted shapes and stitch around the shaped edge, with right sides together. Trim the batting almost back to the seamline, then finish the remaining seam allowances together before turning the glove right side out and finishing the top straight edge with a matching binding. The oven glove here has been quilted with a cable twist pattern (see pages 34 and 93), which suits the long shape of the glove; if you are making a heart-shaped potholder, as seen here, you will find quilting suggestions on the previous page.

RIGHT Small samples of quilting like these, taken from an old strippy quilt, can be turned into an attractive matching set of oven gloves and potholders. The gloves shown here have been quilted with a cable twist pattern.

Knitting Bag

Quilting has here been used to enhance a pretty fabric, and add a soft and luxurious feel to a knitting bag, making it as decorative as it is practical, so it need not be hidden away out of sight between knitting sessions. I also appreciate the fact that this bag doesn't have those straight wooden handles normally associated with knitting bags – the ones that seem to get jammed at odd angles behind chairs, or catch on ribs and doorknobs!

Instead of a specific quilting pattern, there is a backstitched "meander" design with the stitches running in a continuous, randomly curling line across the background of the printed design, but outlining significant elements, such as leaves, buds, and flowers. In order to give the line emphasis, it has been worked in backstitching rather than the usual running stitch. This type of overall pattern is normally associated with flat (two-layer) quilting. The pattern was very popular in the 17th century when quilted bedclothes were often a highly embroidered luxury of the rich; they were a statement of a family's wealth and position in society. Indeed, bed hangings and coverings were often the most expensive single item in a household.

The fabric is particularly attractive – a large-scale floral print. It is lighter than the weight

normally used for upholstery, but a slightly heavier weight of fabric would certainly be perfectly acceptable.

This lighter fabric, however, has the advantage of making stitching easier. The batting is also thin, and the backing layer is of fine, lightweight cotton. A separate lining gives the bag added strength. Depending on the design and particular type of fabric that you find, you might decide to change the embroidery stitch. With a weave that could accommodate stranded embroidery floss, you might – for example – use stem, chain or, if it suited the design, feather stitch.

A strong geometric design might be embellished and enhanced by couched gold thread. Or the thread you use could match the background color. The original choice was in keeping with this fabric, which is no longer available, so you are essentially free to explore your own creativity. The same technique can be used on other small items such as throw pillows, table mats or tea cozies, or even on entire quilts.

As an alternative to this "meander" design, the bag pattern could be used with a solid fabric and quilted with one of the traditional filling patterns such as basketweave.

LEFT   The quilting here has added a luxurious feel to the knitting bag and has also enhanced a pretty floral print fabric. Depending upon the design and type of the fabric used, you can adjust the decorative stitching accordingly.

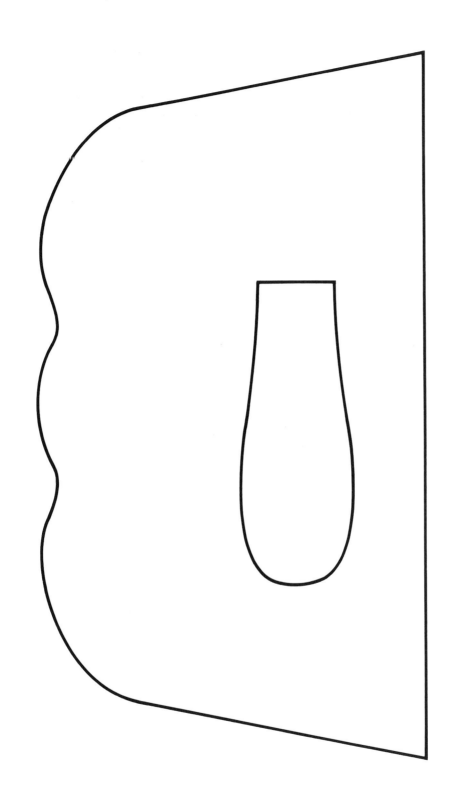

ABILITY LEVEL:
Beginner

SIZE OF FINISHED BAG:
Approximately 18¼ x 11 x 3½ inches

MATERIALS:
• ⅔ yard printed cotton fabric for outside: back, front, sides, handles.

• ⅔ yard of lightweight cotton muslin/calico to back the quilting (not seen when the bag is finished).

• 1 yard solid plain cotton fabric for the inner lining and for the piped edging (2 yards of No. 1 piping cord) and 24 x 36 inches of batting.

• Stranded floss, fine crochet cotton, quilting threads, or other suitable thread, in a color to match or contrast with the fabric (the thread used here was a fine imitation gold thread).

• Pattern pieces: scale up to size (250%) and cut from paper.

CUTTING
Bag front and back Two pieces of main fabric, each measuring 22¼ x 15 inches, and the same of batting and of lightweight cotton.

Handles Four pieces, 15 x 1⅛ inches (seam allowances included).

Sides Using side pattern piece, and adding a ½-inch seam allowance throughout, cut two pieces each from main fabric, and lightweight cotton (also from lining fabric, see below); without adding a seam allowance, cut two pieces from batting.

Piping Cutting on the bias, and bearing in mind that the lining pieces (see below) are cut from the same fabric, cut and join enough strips, each 1½ inches wide, to cover 2 yards of piping cord.

Lining Using the paper pattern pieces and adding ½-inch seam allowances throughout, cut two back/front pieces, two side pieces, and an inner pocket piece (7 inches square).

QUILTING

1 Take the pattern piece for the bag front/back and, centering it on the fabric to leave an even amount of spare fabric on all sides, mark the outline on the right side of one of the pieces of main fabric. Repeat, marking the second front/back piece.

2 Mark quilting lines if you wish.

3 Take one of the prepared top pieces, and assemble it with one of the batting pieces and a cotton backing piece of the same size. Baste thoroughly. Assemble remaining front/back section in the same way.

4 Quilt the meander pattern in backstitch. Alternatively, you could use chain or feather stitch (see page 18), or another embroidery stitch of your choice.

5 Quilt the second back/front piece in the same way.

ASSEMBLING

6 For each side section, place the top and batting together; bring the seam allowance of the main fabric over the edge of the batting and baste in place.

7 Take a backing cotton side section, and turn in the edges all around (½-inch seam allowance). Baste the

turning, then place this piece against the back of prepared top piece. Baste and stitch the two together – near to folded edges – making sure that the backing cannot be seen on the top fabric.

8 Trim each of front/back quilted sections to leave a ½ inch seam allowance beyond the marked outline. With right sides together, pin, baste, and stitch the two parts together along bottom seam. Trim batting close to the stitched seamline.

9 Prepare the handles: press a ¼-inch seam allowance down each long side of each handle strip. Take two pieces and pin them (with the wrong sides together), then topstitch down each long folded edge. Repeat, to prepare the second handle.

10 Take the long bias strip and fold it over the piping cord; baste and stitch, close up against the cord, using the zipper foot of your sewing machine. Trim the covered piping to leave a ½-inch seam allowance.

11 With raw edges matching, lay piping on the right side of the quilted front/back section, pin and baste it in place, all around the edge. Arrange the piping so that the ends meet about halfway down one side edge.

12 Stitch the piping to the quilted section (see step 13 page 61), then trim the batting back close to the seamline.

13 Join the two front/back lining sections along the bottom edge.

14 Turn under a double ¼ inch hem along three sides of the pocket section; along the top, long edge,

turn under ¼ inch and ½ inch and topstitch close to the folded edge.

15 Centering it and placing it 4 inches down from the top of the scalloped edge at one side of the front/back lining piece, topstitch the pocket to the lining (wrong side of pocket to right side of lining).

16 Pin, baste, and stitch the lining side pieces to each side of the main front/back lining section.

17 With right sides together and raw edges matching, pin and baste handles in place at each scalloped (top) edge of quilted front/back section. Stitch along piping seamline, to secure.

18 With right sides together (and handles inside), pin, baste and stitch the lining and the quilted front/back together along the two top scalloped edges, stopping and starting at the side sections. Turn right side out through a side opening.

19 Keeping the lining clear, pin, baste and topstitch side sections to main front/back sections, using zipper foot. Lay side pieces close to back of piping, and stitch close to piping.

20 To finish, turn in the seam allowance of the lining at each top side edge and slipstitch to the top edge of the padded sides.

Pink Strippies

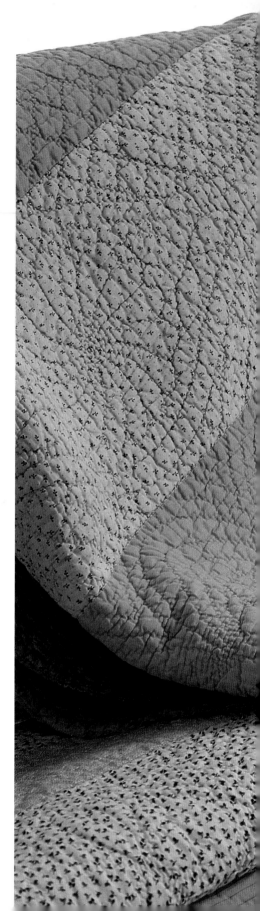

Pink, along with other pastel shades, was popular with English North Country quilters in the 19th century. Sometimes, as with the first of the two quilts described overleaf, the fabric might be predominantly pink on one side and blue on the other, so that the quilt could be used for either a boy or a girl.

In most cases, the quilting patterns used for a strippy are confined to the individual strips, the most striking pattern at the center, and then the corresponding side strips echoing each other out to the edges. It is possible to take a pattern across the strips, but the contrasting

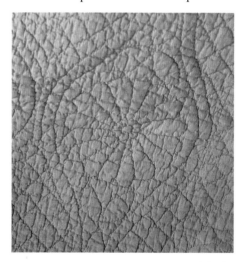

colors tend to break it up visually, and seams make quilting more difficult. Suitable designs, therefore, are of the trailing or repeated border type, such as the twist and trailing feather and leaf patterns found in this collection.

A strippy would make an ideal choice if you are new to quilting and would like to make a full-scale quilt, but have only so far made smaller items. Traditionally, the strips were joined before quilting, but you may find it easier to use the quilt-as-you-go technique described overleaf, in which the strips are quilted separately before being joined. The second of these two quilts is unusual in having an even number of strips and only two quilting patterns, which makes it an ideal beginner's project.

RIGHT Delicate pinks and subtly patterned white fabrics provide a unifying factor in this collection of 19th-century quilts from the north of England.
ABOVE The soft colors allow the quilting designs to be seen clearly.

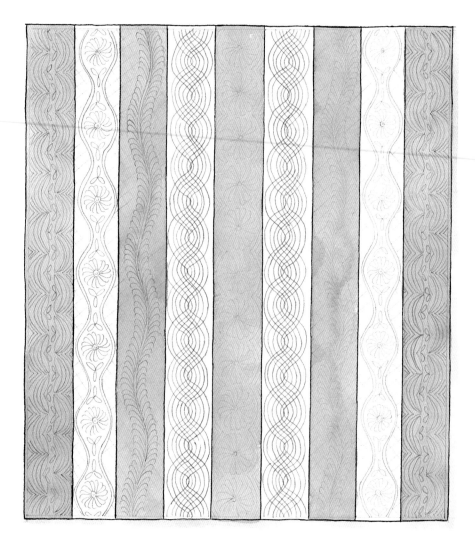

ABILITY LEVEL:
Beginner/Intermediate

SIZE OF FINISHED QUILT:
80 x 86 inches

MATERIALS:
• You can use printed or solid cotton fabrics for the strips; in the original quilt, the pink fabric is plain, but the white fabric has an unobtrusive pattern of small, dark navy blue sprigs. There are five pink strips and four white ones. You will need 5 yards of pink fabric (this assumes a standard fabric width of 45 inches, but there would be considerable wastage, so try to find a fabric 60 inches wide, where you would need 2½ yards of fabric). For the white strips, you will need 2½ yards of solid or sprigged white fabric.

• 5 yards of blue fabric – a clear blue, very similar in tone to the pink, has been used for the back of the quilt, providing a striking and unusual contrast with the front; if you feel that this might look too "contrasty" or "baby boy/girl," you could either use a plain white fabric or the pink.

• 92 x 88 inches of batting.

CUTTING
Back of quilt From blue backing fabric, cut two 9½ x 88-inch strips; six 10 x 88-inch strips, and one measuring 10½ x 88 inches.

Strips From pink fabric, cut four 10 x 88 inch strips, and one measuring 10½ x 88 inches.

From white sprigged fabric, cut two 9½ x 88-inch strips, and two 10 x 8-inch strips.

Batting Cut two 9½ x 88-inch strips; six 10 x 88-inch strips, and one measuring 10½ x 88 inches.

MARKING
1 You will need five templates (enlarge all by 250%) for this quilt, used as follows (the strips are numbered from left to right): strips 1 and 9 (pink), inverted hammocks; strips 2 and 8 (white), roses and petals; strips 3 and 7 (pink), trailing feather pattern; strips 4 and 6 (white), twist; and center strip 5 (pink), large rose.

2 Take the pink fabric for strip 1, measuring 10 x 88 inches, and mark a line ½ inch in from the raw edge down one long side, stopping 1½ inches short of the raw edge at each end. In the same way, mark a line 1½ inches from the raw edge down the remaining long side (this will be the outer quilted line down the side edge of the quilt) and across each short end, making a long rectangle. Take the second strip of the same width and mark it in the same way, but place the wider margin on the opposite long edge, to make a mirror image. No quilting lines should run over this border line.

3 On strip 1, measure from the marked edges and draw a faint guide-line down the center of the strip. Take the hammock template and mark hammocks, linking at the corners, down one side of the line. Mark hammocks down the other side of the line, staggering them so that the corners of the hammocks on one side of the line meet at the centers of the hammocks down the other side. On this and all subsequent strips, it is best to start marking at the middle of each strip and work out to each end. Take the leaf template and mark leaves between the hammocks, as shown.

4 Between the hammocks, on each side of the center line, are three lines of contour quilting, echoing the outer lines of the hammocks. You can make a template for these lines, but it may be easiest to mark them in by hand.

5 Mark strip 9 in the same manner.

6 Take the white top fabric for strip 2, measuring 9½ x 88 inches, and mark rose and petal repeat patterns down the center of the strip. Take a quilter's ruler, and mark a pattern of square-diamonds, the lines set 1 inch apart, to fill in the spaces at each side of the marked pattern. Leave a ½ inch seam allowance unmarked on each long edge of the strip and mark a border line 1½ inches from the raw edge at each end.

7 Mark the corresponding strip 8 in the same way.

8 Take the pink strip 3, measuring 10 x 88 inches, and mark the trailing feather pattern down the strip. Crosshatch with the 1-inch square-diamond filling pattern at each side, again leaving a margin unmarked all around the edges (see step 6).

9 Mark the corresponding strip 7 in the same way.

10 Take the white strip 4, measuring 10 x 88 inches, and mark it with the twist pattern, making sure that you leave a margin unmarked all around the edges (see step 6).

11 Take the center, pink strip, measuring 10½ x 88 inches, and mark the large rose pattern, leaving an unmarked margin as usual.

QUILTING

12 First assemble the three layers of each strip in order (batting and backing fabric are the same size as the top fabric) and label them – you may find it helpful to roll up the strips of batting, backing fabric and main fabric for each individual strip and keep each set in a separate bag, labeled with the strip number and the quilting pattern.

13 Take the marked top, batting, and backing fabric for strip 1 and assemble the layers (see page 17), basting thoroughly.

14 Quilt all but the outer marked line, taking care not to extend the quilting beyond this line.

15 Repeat, until each strip has been quilted.

16 Lay the quilted strips out flat and work out a practical joining

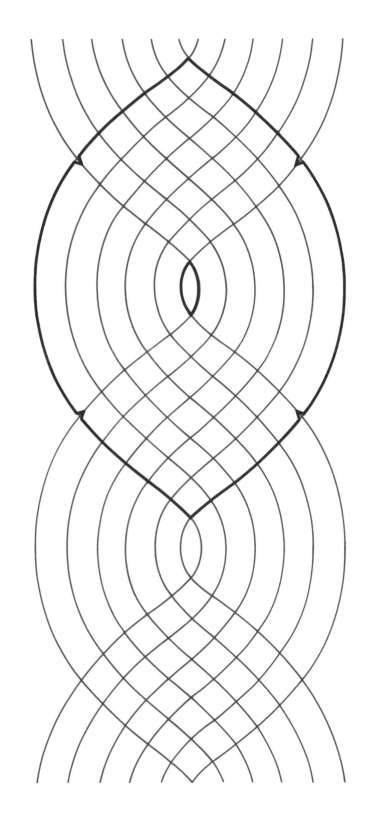

sequence; for example, into pairs and then larger units. Take the first pair of strips to be joined; fold back the backing and batting layers and, with right sides together, stitch along the length, joining the quilt top layers only, and taking a ½-inch seam allowance. Trim, and then press.

17 Open the two strips flat and trim surplus batting until the edges butt up against each other. Stitch the edges together, using either feather or herringbone stitch (see page 18).

18 Bring one edge of the backing fabric over the joined batting layer; turn the other edge under and hand-stitch, using either a matching thread and a slipstitch, or a decorative feather stitch and a contrasting thread.

19 Join all strips together in this fashion to complete the top, then quilt the outer marked border line.

20 Trim the batting to a scant ½ inch beyond the quilted line. Trim the top and backing to extend ⅛ inch beyond the batting. Fold in the top and backing, so the folded edge is ½ inch clear of the outer quilted line, and stitch the two together around the edge, close to the foldline.

SECOND PINK STRIPPY

Note: The strippy described here is to be made up and quilted in the traditional manner. You could, however, easily use the quilt-as-you-go method described for the previous strippy.

ABILITY LEVEL:
Beginner/Intermediate

SIZE OF FINISHED QUILT:
85 x 92 inches

MATERIALS:
• Use printed or solid cotton fabrics for the strips. In the original quilt, the pink fabric has a mottled background of pale pink, striped with narrow lines of deeper candy pink; the white fabric has a faded pattern of tiny blue dots. You will need 5⅜ yards of each using fabric of the standard width of 45 inches; if you can find suitable fabric at least 50 inches wide, you will need only 2⅔ yards of each fabric.

• 5⅜ yards of solid or patterned fabric for the backing. The backing fabric used for the original quilt has a pastel pattern of pinkish-purple paisley teardrops against a white background, with the pattern being sufficiently small and subdued to allow the quilting lines to remain clearly visible.

• 89 x 96 inches of batting

• Flexible curve – this is optional, but it would be a very useful tool for drawing the trailing leaf pattern, and you would probably find it useful for future quilting designs and other drawing purposes. Available from artstores supply, a flexible curve is a long strip with straight-edged sides against which you can draw (like a

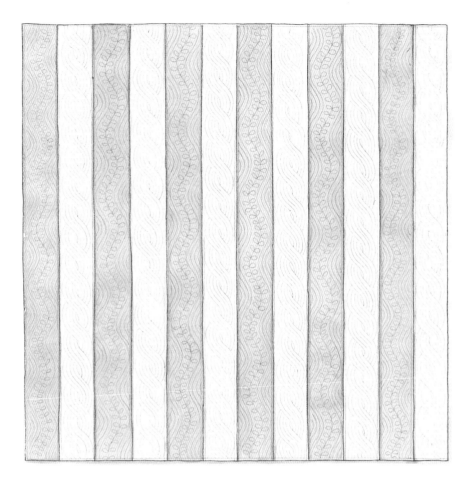

ruler) but it can be molded into a curve and will hold its shape.

CUTTING
Back of quilt Two pieces of backing fabric, each 45 x 96 inches.

Strips From pink striped fabric, cut six strips, each 96 inches long; five are 8 inches wide, the remaining one is 10 inches wide. From white fabric, cut six strips, as above.

ASSEMBLING
Note: you can either mark the strips individually, before assembling the quilt top, or after, as described below. If you are marking the strips

before assembly, mark a line 2½ inches from the raw edge at the top and bottom of each strip, and leave ½ inch allowances unmarked down all ten of the narrower strips. For the two wide strips, which will be at the sides, mark a line 2½ inches from the raw edge down the side which will be the side edge of the quilt (the left-hand edge of the pink strip and right-hand edge of the white one); other margins are the same as for the other strips.

1 Taking ½ inch seam allowances, stitch all the strips together – alternating pink strips with white ones – and setting the wider strips at the edges of the quilt. To even out

any stretching in the fabrics, stitch seams alternately from top to bottom and then from the bottom to the top end of the quilt. Press all seams open.

2 With a ½ inch seam allowance, join the backing fabric together on one long edge and press the seam open.

MARKING
3 Lay the assembled quilt top on a flat surface, and smooth out any wrinkles in the material. Then – using pins or some other marker that is easily removable – mark a line across the center. This line should divide all of the strips in two across the width.

4 Mark lines along all four sides of the top, 2½ inches from the raw edge. This marks the outer edge of the quilting patterns.

5 Only two patterns were used for this quilt: a trailing leaf pattern and a twist. The trailing leaf may either be drawn freehand, with a flexible curve to make the curving line, or – alternatively – with templates. As each pattern is repeated several times, it might be a good idea to make the templates from plastic; both the twist and the trailing leaf are much-loved traditional patterns; the oval template used for the twist pattern can be used for many variations, and templates can be kept for re-use on later projects.

6 Mark the twist pattern down each white strip. For each strip, start at the marked center line and work out to each end, making sure that the pattern is balanced. Make sure that the twist pattern runs down the center of each strip; bear in mind that the outer strip will finish at the marked line, so the pattern here should be centered between the seamline and the marked outer line.

7 Mark the trailing leaf stem down each pink strip, again starting from the marked center line, to ensure that you have an even number of repeats and start and finish at the same point. For each strip, either using a template or a flexible curve, draw the curving shape, with a stem down the center. Each curve should not come any closer than 2¼ inches to the seamline, and a complete curve from one side of the strip and back to the same side covers a distance of 14 inches down the length of the strip.

As was the case with the twist design, make sure that the stem runs down the center of each strip; when marking the outer strip, you should bear in mind that the marked line denotes the outer quilted line around the finished quilt, so the stem here should be centered between the inner seamline and the marked outer line.

8 Freehand or using the template, mark leaves in slightly staggered pairs along the stem. As can be seen on the original quilt, there are about 9 leaves on each side of the stem within each complete curve.

9 The twist pattern fills the appropriate strips with no further need for filling patterns. For the strips marked with the trailing leaf pattern, also mark lines of contour quilting, almost to the edge of the strip, as shown. (Each strip has a line of quilting ⅛ inch away from the seamline on each side, so it is important not to cross this line.) These contour lines echo precisely the central curving line of the "stem." As before, you can either use a template or a flexible curve, keeping this in the shape already used for the main stem. Draw four contour lines within the hollow of each curve, spacing them ⅞ inch apart, with the first roughly ½ inch from the tip of the leaf in the deepest part of the curve.

QUILTING

10 Take the marked top, batting, and backing fabric and assemble the layers.

11 Quilt a line (not marked) on each side of each strip seamline, ⅛ inch away from the seamline.

12 Quilt the twist pattern, and quilt the trailing leaf pattern. When

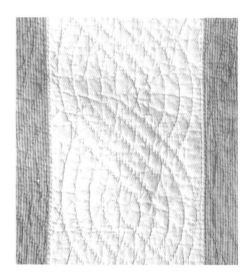

quilting the contour lines of the trailing leaf pattern, quilt a second line, ⅛ inch away from each line (nearer to the outside of the strip) so all contour lines are in fact double-quilted.

13 Quilt the marked edging line around the quilt.

14 When you have finished quilting, trim the batting back to within ½ inch of the outer quilted line.

15 Trim the top and backing to ½ inch of the batting, and finish with a folded edge (see page 19).

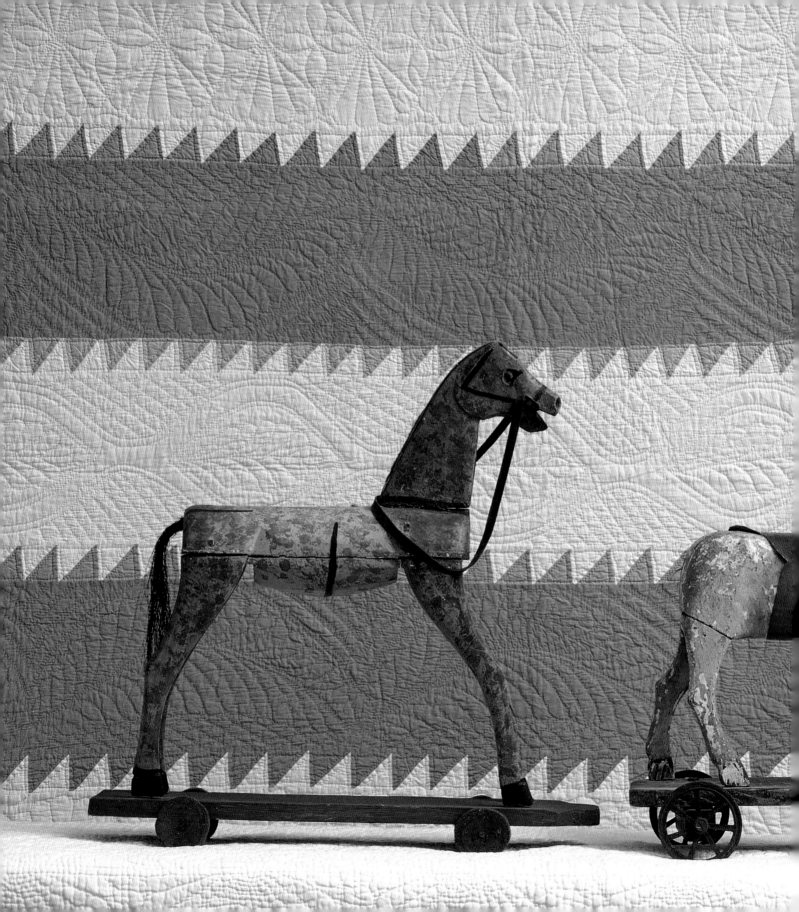

Blue & White Strippy

This handsome quilt surely looks as fresh and bold as the day its maker sat back with pride after putting in the final stitch! Designed, marked, and stitched by an able quilter, this is no run-of-the-mill strippy. The little feathers of the central design are echoed by the curved feathers of the adjacent blue strips, which contribute a sense of flow; this is reinforced by the contour quilting of the infill pattern, which points out toward the edges of the quilt.

Strip quilts with patchwork generally alternate strips of large, simple patchwork with plain quilted fabric, whereas here the patchwork is innovatively confined to sashing strips that link and emphasize the broad, quilted pieces.

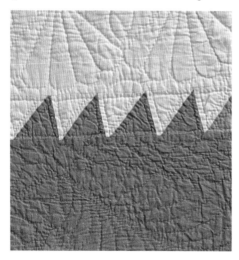

The strong, attractive blue has lasted well, but take care when choosing fabrics to test that the blue is colorfast (see page 14). Many blue cottons contain indigo dye that has not been set effectively, and it would be heart-breaking to spoil such a handsome quilt with inferior fabrics. The patchwork strips leave a narrow margin for folding in the edge at the top and bottom of the quilt; it may help if you add strips of spare white fabric to the top and bottom of each patchwork sashing strip and to the side edges.

LEFT AND ABOVE The beautifully and evenly stitched patchwork strips enhance the quilted strips of this unusually sumptuous and elaborate 19th-century strippy from the North of England.

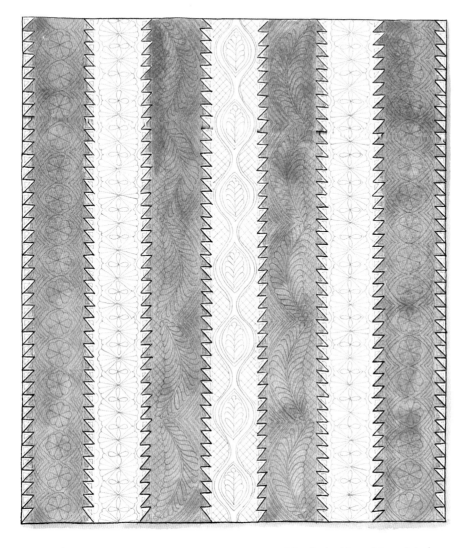

ABILITY LEVEL:
Intermediate/advanced

SIZE OF FINISHED COVER:
94½ x 84 inches

MATERIALS:
• 3⅔ yards of blue cotton fabric, and the same of white, for the strips and the patchwork.

• 5½ yards of solid or printed cotton fabric for the backing; the quilting does not blend with the strong pattern used for the backing of the original quilt and is almost swamped by it, but it would be possible to choose a very different color or pattern for the backing fabric, and one that is more in keeping with the quilting design, to make the cover reversible.

• 96½ x 86 inches of batting.

• Templates for quilting (enlarge by 250%) and photocopied grid sheets (optional, see step 1).

CUTTING

Back of cover Two pieces, 96½ x 43½ inches, backing fabric.

Strips Four strips, each 95½ x 10½ inches, from blue fabric; three strips, each 95½ x 10 inches, white fabric.

Patchwork Either 160 squares of blue fabric and the same of white, each measuring 3¼ x 3⅛ inches, cut each square in half diagonally, to give 320 triangles of each color; or use the speedy patchwork method described in steps 1–3 below.

PIECING

NOTE: You can either mark the main quilted strips individually, before assembling the quilt top, or after, as described below. If you are marking the strips before assembly, remember to leave ½-inch seam allowances down the strips, and at the top and bottom of each.

1 Prepare patchwork sashing strips. The patchwork strips of the original quilt were all machine-sewn, which is more durable than hand-stitching. You can either cut the triangles and stitch them individually, in the traditional way, or use the method described here: draw up a grid of 3⅛ inch squares on paper, dividing each square diagonally into triangles, as shown. Using lightweight paper in the copier, take enough photocopies to give a total of 160 squares (320 triangles). Photocopies can stretch a tiny bit, so to keep patches all the same size, use only photocopies, not the original grid drawing.

2 Cut one piece of blue fabric and one piece of white the same size as your paper grid. Lay the fabrics with right

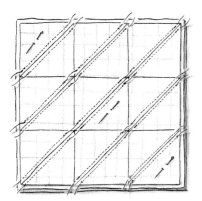

sides together and pin grid on top. Stitching through all three layers, stitch ¼ inch on each side of the marked diagonal lines and backstitch before and after you cross each vertical and diagonal (cutting) line. On most sewing machines, the space between the outer edge of the foot and the point of the needle is ¼ inch, so all you have to do is to keep the marked diagonal line precisely in line with the outer edge of the sewing foot.

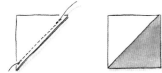

3 Repeat until you have used up all your grids, then cut along all the marked lines. Tear away the paper from each pair of joined triangles, and press seams open.

4 Making sure that white and blue always alternate, join two squares; repeat until you have 80 pairs. Join the pairs into fours, and then the fours into eights.

5 Then join two 8-square strips, and then two more; join these together, and add a fifth strip, to make one 40-square sashing strip.

Make seven more sashing strips in the same way.

6 Pin and stitch a sashing strip to each long side of each 10½ inch blue strip. To avoid wrinkles, take care to even out any excess fabric on each side along the whole length. Note that the seam allowance on the patchwork is ¼ inch, while the allowance on the wholecloth strips is ½ inch.

7 Join a pieced/blue strip to each side

of a white strip, again leaving a ½-inch allowance on the patchwork and a ½-inch allowance on the wholecloth strips, then join these sections, setting the remaining white strip in the middle. Stitch seams alternately from top to bottom and bottom to top, to even out any stretching in the fabrics. Press all seams open.

8 Join the two pieces of backing fabric down one long side, taking ½-inch seam allowances. Press the seam allowances to one side.

MARKING

9 Lay the assembled quilt top on a flat surface, smoothing out any wrinkles and, using pins or an easily removable marker, mark a line across the middle, dividing all strips in two across the width.

10 Mark a line across the top and bottom, ¼ inch from raw edges of the whole strips (½ inch from the edges of pieced strips); mark down the sides, ½ inch from raw edges. This marks the outer edge of the quilting patterns.

11 Always starting from the middle and working out to the top and bottom, mark the strip quilting patterns, starting with the central, white strip.

First mark the central little feather motifs and surrounding "flat-iron" frames, then fill in the spaces outside the outer bellows-style frame with a square-diamond pattern, the lines set ¾ inch apart.

12 Next mark the two adjacent blue strips with the curved feather. The feathers curl outward, away from the central strip, and meet tip to tail. In the spaces next to the central strip, mark the chevron pattern. Only mark one of each pair of double lines, the second, parallel line lies ¼ inch away, and the distance can be judged by eye. The spaces on the other side (within the curl of the feather) are filled

with the same square-diamond pattern as the central strip.

13 The next two (white) strips are marked with a pattern formed by linked fan shapes and four-petaled flowers (like the American pumpkin seed pattern), with just a half-circle filling the gaps left by the curves of the fans. Draw the fans first, then the flowers, and finally the half-circles.

14 Mark the outermost strips with roses, set along the center, 1 inch apart, and fill in with chevrons (stitched as single lines) and ovals.

QUILTING

15 Take the marked top, batting, and backing fabric and assemble the layers (see page 17).

16 Contour quilt each patchwork triangle with a line of stitching ¼ inch in from the seamline.

17 Also quilt all marked quilting lines. When quilting the chevron filling pattern of the curled feather strips, remember to quilt a second line, ¼ inch away from each line (nearer to the outside of the strip) so that all these lines are in fact double-quilted.

18 Quilt the marked edging line around the quilt.

19 When you have finished quilting, trim the batting back to within a scant ¼ inch of the outer quilted line.

20 Trim the top and backing to ½ inch of the quilted edge, and finish with a folded edge (see page 19).

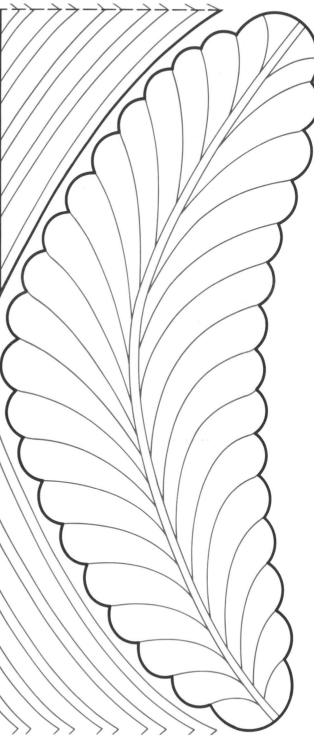

Red & White Strippy

Red and white was a color combination much favored for patchwork and appliqué covers by quiltmakers in North America and Britain, as can be seen in this varied collection of 19th-century red and white quilts.

White cotton was inexpensive, and therefore used in almost all quilts. Turkey red dye, which had been used in the East for many centuries, became available in the early 19th century. This dye was both strong and permanent, and the resulting red fabrics offered quilters a strong color contrast with the white that could withstand washing and normal wear and tear.

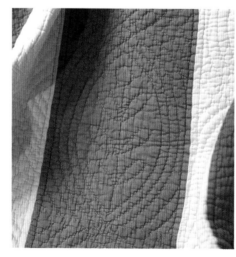

The quilts in this particular collection include three strippies. One of these strippies has been detailed overleaf, and there is also a star design, very similar to that of the pink and white star quilt, which can be found on page 77.

The strippy described here is the width of a single bed – including an overlap at each side. If you require a wider cover, the size can easily be altered; this can be achieved either by adding more strips to the design, or by slightly increasing the size of the quilting patterns to fit a wider measure.

Equally, there is no need to feel restricted to the particular combination of designs seen here. As previously mentioned in the book, suitable designs for strippies are of the repeated or trailing border type – the twist and trailing feather and leaf patterns; the quilting patterns for strippies are normally confined to the individual strips rather than crossing the strips.

Nevertheless, if you are adding to the strips or if you would like to vary the patterns more, there are many other traditional strip patterns given in this book. These include the designs for the other strippies on pages 34 and 45, and many of the border patterns to be found in the wholecloth section. The fan border of the quilt found on page 99, for example, could quite easily be adapted to make an attractive strippy design simply by turning alternate fans to face in the opposite direction.

RIGHT   Red and white, as seen in this collection of quilts, has always been a popular color combination for patchwork and appliqué covers in North America and Britain.

ABOVE   Detail of one of the strippies showing the leaf quilting pattern.

red fabric). 82 x 89 inches of batting (includes extra, to allow for shrinkage during quilting).

• Templates (enlarge by 235%).

CUTTING

Strips From white fabric, cut four strips 9½ x 89 inches; from red fabric, cut two strips 11 x 89 inches, and three strips 10 x 89 inches.

Back of cover From white fabric, cut two pieces 21 x 89 inches, and one 42 x 89 inches.

JOINING AND MARKING

Note: you can either mark the strips individually, before assembling the quilt top, or after, as described below. If marking strips before assembly, first mark a line 2½ inches from raw edge at the top and bottom of each strip, and mark a line 1 inch in from raw edge down each side of all strips, except for the two wider (11-inch) red strips. For these strips (the sides of the finished quilt), mark a line 1-inch from the raw edge down the inner side and 2½ inches from the raw edge down the side that will be the side edge of the quilt. Mark patterns as described below.

1 Taking ½ inch seam allowances, stitch all the strips together, alternating red strips with white, and setting the wider red strips at the edges of the quilt. To even out any stretching in the fabrics, stitch seams alternately from top to bottom and then from the bottom to the top end of the quilt. Press all seams open.

2 Taking ½ inch seam allowances, join the three pieces of backing fabric together, setting the widest

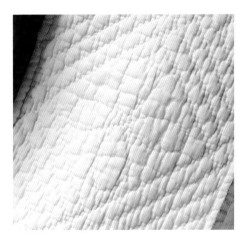

ABILITY LEVEL:
Beginner/Intermediate

SIZE OF FINISHED QUILT:
78 x 85 inches

MATERIALS:
• 7½ yards of white cotton fabric, for strips and backing.

• 5 yards of red cotton fabric, for strips (this assumes fabric is 45 inches wide; if you can find fabric 56 inches wide, you will only need 2½ yards of

piece in the center. Then press the seams open.

3 Lay the assembled quilt top on a flat surface, smoothing out wrinkles. Then, using pins or a removable marker, mark a line across the center, dividing all strips in two across width.

4 Mark lines along all four sides of the top, 2½ inches from the raw edge. This marks the outer edge of the quilting patterns. Also draw lines ½ inch out from the seamline on each side of every seam, stopping at the marked outer quilting lines at the top and bottom. The strip quilting patterns are contained within these lines. When marking the strip patterns, always start at the marked (horizontal) center line and work to the top and bottom, to make sure that pattern repeats are evenly balanced.

5 The pattern of the center strip is based on semicircles with radii of 3⅜ inches, 3⅛ inches, 2⅝ inches, 2⅛ inches, 1⅞ inches, 1⅜ inches, and ¼ inch. These sets of circles are arranged in matching pairs, with a ⅛ inch space between them down the center of the quilt. The star-like shape between each two pairs of circles is filled with square-diamonds, the lines set ⅞ inch apart. You can either make templates, or make only one template for the larger half-circle, drawing the others by hand. As an alternative, you could use a pair of compasses, setting the point for the first circle at the intersection of the horizontal center line and one of the marked side lines.

6 Use the wavy line and chevrons templates to mark strips 1, 4, 6, and 9 (reading from left to right).

7 Strips 2 and 8 are filled with flowers and crossed lines. There are 11 flowers in all, spaced 7½ inches apart, from flower center to flower center. Start with the center flower, then set five on each side. Spacing the lines ½ inch apart, surround the flowers with sets of three parallel lines, so that each is framed in a diamond-set square with sides measuring 4¼ inches. Fill in the empty triangles with sets of three triangles, again ½ inch apart. You will find a quilter's rule and a square useful here.

8 To finish, mark the pattern for strips 3 and 7, again starting by drawing the first motif at the (horizontal) center, and working out in both directions. Note that all flowers are placed with their heads nearest to the top of the quilt. Fill in each side space with two chevrons, echoing the curving flat-iron frames.

QUILTING

9 Take the marked top, batting, and backing fabric and assemble the layers (see page 17).

10 Quilt all the marked lines, including the marked edging line around the quilt.

11 When you have finished quilting, trim the batting back to within ½-inch of the outer quilted line.

12 Trim the top and backing to ½-inch of the batting, and finish with a folded edge (see page 19).

Strippy Baby Quilt

The maker of this pretty baby quilt hedged her bets by alternating strips of pink and blue. She finished with a separate binding cut from blue fabric (see page 17), but otherwise this pretty little strippy was made in the same way as those on pages 34, 45, and 50. The finished quilt is formed from eight strips and measures approximately 35½ x 36¾ inches, but the number, width and length of the strips can be varied to fit a particular bed, crib, or cradle.

The quilting pattern is a simple lined cable twist, and because the strips are narrow – approximately 4½ inches wide – the twist design is

taken across two strips at a time. A small-scale quilt of this type offers an ideal opportunity to experiment with a range of twist or cable designs; all are made with an eye-shaped template, though the internal patterns vary considerably. The feathered twist, in which one side of the twist is a curling feather, is an attractive variation. If you are making your own template, you might like to use a small coin, in the traditional manner, to draw the outer rounded shapes of the feathering. The Weardale chain, named after a region famous for its quilting, was another popular twist pattern from the North of England; the twists in this design are filled with simple flower shapes.

RIGHT In colors of pink and blue – traditional for a girl or boy – this early 20th-century strippy can be easily adapted to fit a particular child's bed. ABOVE The quilting pattern is a simple lined cable twist.

Embroidered Baby Quilt

In the 1930s, when this charming crib or buggy quilt was made, baskets were a popular motif – on printed fabrics, embroideries, and wallpapers, and in the form of brooches. The top and backing are of cotton sateen, which offered the sheen of silk with the washability that is essential for a baby quilt. Various polished fabrics were – and still are – used for quilts, including Shantung silk and mercerized cotton. The disadvantage of the latter is that the glaze tends to wear away with washing. Rayon, which is made from wood pulp, was discovered before World War I, and during that war it was found that the chemical sprayed on the wings of fighter planes had the effect of giving rayon a silk-like sheen. However, as with other artificial fibers, rayon is less satisfactory for quilting than fabrics made from cotton or silk.

In theory, the quilting lines should have been closer than they are in this design, to prevent the batting from shifting between the layers, but the filling has held its place remarkably well, despite the ravages of four different babies. The color, however, has faded a little with age. It was a common practice to make crib quilts reversible, one side pink and one side blue, though in this case the same color was used for both sides.

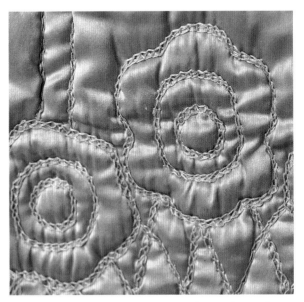

Unusually, here the quilting lines have been reworked in chain stitch, and although the more frequently used hand-quilting stitch is even running stitch, other embroidery stitches can be added. Flat quilts (those with only two layers) of the 17th and 18th centuries were frequently decorated with a wide variety of surface embroidery stitches, including satin, split, stem, long and short, chain, and bullion stitches. Backstitch offers an alternative means of holding padded quilting layers together, producing continuous lines that give an effect somewhat akin to that of machine quilting.

LEFT AND ABOVE   This late 1930s satin quilt is of a size to fit an old-fashioned buggy or a small crib. The quilted lines have been covered with chain stitch, on both sides of this unusual quilt.

ABILITY LEVEL:
Intermediate

SIZE OF FINISHED COVER:
32½ x 22 inches

MATERIALS:
• 2 yards of shiny cotton or silk fabric – for the top and backing – and for the piped edging; if you would like to have a contrasting backing, you will need ¾ yard each of the top and backing fabrics, as well as 1 yard of the fabric chosen for the covered piping.

• 34½ x 24 inches of batting (this includes extra, to allow for shrinkage during quilting); the batting used was slightly thicker than than the relatively thin type normally used for whole-cloth quilts. This is more difficult to stitch, but of course is more cozy for a baby, and it gives a greater degree of "loft" (the contrast between the flattened lines of quilting and the raised areas between), which enhances the design.

• 3¼ yards of No. 1 piping cord.

• 3 skeins of stranded floss, in a color to match the fabric.

• Quilting thread or strong sewing cotton in the same shade as the stranded floss.

• Quilting/embroidery design (enlarge by 400%) and tracing paper/black felt marker pen. See step 1.

CUTTING
Front and back of quilt Two pieces of fabric, each 34½ x 24 inches.

Piping Cutting on the bias, cut and join enough strips, making each 1½ inches wide, to cover 3¼ yards of piping cord when joined.

MARKING

1 Instead of making templates, it would be simpler to trace the whole design onto the fabric. Scale up the design to its full size, and copy it onto tracing paper. Run over the lines, if necessary, with a black felt marker pen, to make them stand out clearly.

2 The traced design is placed under the top fabric and copied; this can be done in several ways. If you can see the black outlines through the fabric, the task is relatively easy. Simply lay the design on a suitable flat surface and secure the corners with drafting tape to hold it firm.

3 Next, lay the top fabric, right side up, over the design, and again tape the corners, and if necessary the sides, to hold it firm. Finally – using the marker of your choice (a quilter's pen, or perhaps a well-sharpened pencil in a color close to but distinguishable from the fabric color) – trace the design outlines on the fabric. If you cannot see the outlines, use a light box, or tape the design and fabric to a window and use natural daylight. Another option is to make your own light box by placing a low-heat light under a glass-topped table.

4 When you have marked the design, draw a frame around it measuring 32½ x 22 inches; make sure that this is spaced an equal distance from the edge of the design on each side. This marks the outer edge of the quilt.

QUILTING AND EMBROIDERING

5 Take the marked top, batting, and backing fabric and assemble the layers (see page 17), basting thoroughly.

6 Start by quilting along the marked design lines in the ordinary way, using the quilting thread. Do not quilt around the outer marked frame that shows the finished edge of the quilt.

7 When all the design lines have been quilted, at this point you can now embroider over them. If you find it easier to work with the fabric in the hand at this stage, it can be removed from the frame.

8 Using two strands of floss in the needle, and going closely along the quilting lines, covering the original stitches, embroider the design in chain stitch. Pick up the top fabric only; it doesn't matter if the needle passes through the batting to some extent, but the back of the chain stitch, which looks like a backstitch, should not be visible on the other side of the work.

9 Embroider the other side of the quilt with chain stitch also, to make the quilt reversible.

FINISHING

10 Take the long bias strip and fold it over the piping cord; baste and stitch, close up against the cord, using the zipper foot of your sewing machine.

11 Trim all three layers to leave a ½ inch seam allowance beyond the outer marked (unquilted) line, and trim the covered piping to the same allowance. Remove all basting stitches, and pin back the backing fabric around the edges, so that it is clear of the front of the quilt and batting.

12 With raw edges matching, pin and baste the piping around the front cover and batting, leaving the backing clear and basting the piping in place along the marked outer line. Arrange the piping so that the ends meet about halfway down one side edge of the quilt.

13 At the join, trim the covering of the piping to a ¼-inch overlap at each end and unpick the stitching for about 1 inch; fold under the allowance at one end and lap this over the other, unfolded allowance. Unravel the cord ends, trimming one or two back on each side to reduce bulk, and twist them together, making a few stitches to hold them. Fold the covering back over the cord, and baste the join.

14 Stitch the piping to the front cover and batting, then trim the batting back close to the seamline.

15 Unpin the backing fabric and turn under a ½ inch seam allowance all around. Slipstitch the folded edge of the backing fabric to the front, close to the piping cord.

Country Quilt

The chief attraction of this 19th-century French country quilt lies in the lovely rich fabric of the top cover, rather than the actual quilting pattern. French quilters made many elaborately quilted covers, including solid-colored wholecloth quilts, and the elaborate wedding quilts known as *courtepointes*. The latter were made from scarves printed on three sides, with a matching strip of fabric added to make up the fourth side. However, other quilts, including the one seen here, were designed primarily for warmth. These had far simpler quilting patterns and longer, more spaced-out stitches.

Here, instead of a complex pattern, the quilting design has been kept to a minimum; the aim is simply to hold the three layers together. A quilt like this would make an excellent practice piece for a beginner, particularly as quilting patterns do not stand out very clearly against a highly patterned fabric, and therefore small mistakes would not really be noticeable.

The pattern of this quilt is very simple: the square-diamond design that can be found in certain areas on almost every quilt in this book. Depending on the fabric pattern, there are other popular filling patterns that could be used, and several of these options are given here.

LEFT The attraction of this 19th-century French quilt lies as much in the beautiful fabric as it does in the quilting pattern itself.

ABOVE The quilting design — the square-diamond — is not complex.

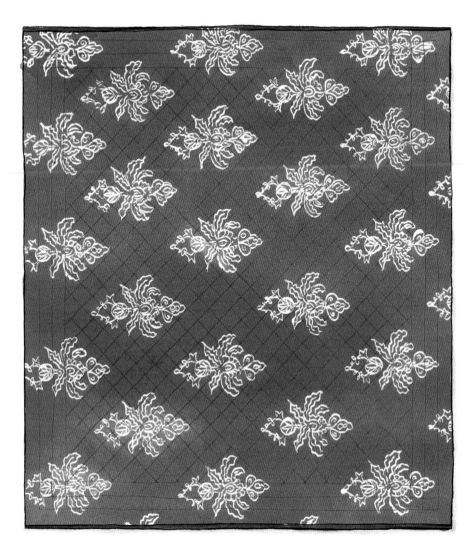

ABILITY LEVEL:
Beginner

SIZE OF FINISHED QUILT:
78¼ x 89 inches

MATERIALS:

Note: quantities given below, and the cutting instructions, are for a quilt cut from fabric 45 inches wide; if you are making this quilt from an antique length of fabric, you might have to alter the size and piece the lengths

together in a different way. Try to make sure that the seams of the backing do not fall in the same place as the front seams, as you will then have to stitch through four layers of fabric, in addition to the batting, when stitching across seams.

• 5¼ yards of patterned cotton or other suitable fabric, for quilt top.

• 5¼ yards of solid fabric for backing (the backing is turned to the front at

the top and bottom of the quilt, so it should make an attractive match or contrast with the top fabric).

• 82¼ x 93 inches of batting (this includes extra, to allow for shrinkage during quilting). The batting used for this quilt was thicker than that used for the other quilts in this book; if you are a relative newcomer to quilting, it might be a good idea to experiment by stitching small sample pieces of varying thickness before starting this project.

CUTTING

Front cover From patterned fabric, cut two pieces 21½ x 93 inches, and one 41¼ x 93 inches.

Back cover From solid fabric, cut two pieces 20½ x 93 inches, and one piece 43¼ x 93 inches.

JOINING AND MARKING

1 First assemble the pieces for the front. Taking ½-inch seam allowances, join the three lengths cut for the top, setting the wide piece in the middle. Press both seams open.

2 Join the lengths cut for the back in the same way.

3 Press the top fabric and lay it out carefully on a flat surface (see page 17), ready to mark the design. Start by marking central vertical and horizontal guidelines, dividing the top into four quarters. Do this either by pressing or basting, as the guidelines should be easily removable so that they will not be visible on the finished quilt.

4 To mark the quilting design, first draw the outer limit of the quilting – a rectangle measuring 78 x 88¼ inches

– making sure that opposite sides are spaced equally from the center. (To check, fold the rectangle diagonally each way – the diagonals should be the same length and cross at the marked center.)

5 Within this, mark a second rectangle 2¼ inches from the first.

6 Within the second rectangle, draw two more, successively 2¼ inches further in. The lines forming these rectangles cross over at the corners, to finish at the edge of the second rectangle, as shown.

7 Fill the center with the filling pattern of your choice (see below), bearing in mind the way in which a particular quilting pattern might complement the fabric of your choice. When deciding on the scale of your quilting pattern, take into account that a thicker batting makes stitching more difficult, so very closely set lines might create problems if you are using a thick filling.

QUILTING

8 Assemble the three layers – backing, batting, and marked top (see page 17).

9 Quilt all marked lines, including the outer marked line.

10 When you have finished quilting, trim the batting back to within a scant ⅜ inch of the outer quilted line.

11 Trim the top and backing fabrics down the sides to within ½ inch of the batting. Then bring the top fabric over the edge of the batting, and turn in the edge of the backing fabric to meet it. Pin and baste.

12 Along the top and bottom of the quilt, trim the front cover to the same level as the batting. Trim the backing to within ¾ inch of the batting and front cover.

13 Topstitch the front and back together neatly down the sides, stitching close to the folded edges.

14 At the top and bottom edges, fold the backing under for a scant ⅜ inch. Bring the folded edges neatly over to the front of the quilt to meet the outermost quilted line, and neatly slipstitch in place.

FILLER PATTERNS:

Shells
To add interest, the shell outlines can be filled in a variety of ways; the variation shown here was found on a Devon quilt of about 1866.

Waves
This was much favored by Irish quilters as a filling pattern and can be found on many American quilts.

Wineglass / teacup
Where this is to be used (as here) as an all-over pattern rather than a filling to be contrasted with other motifs, the circles can be as large as the batting will allow. An alternative template for this pattern is made from four of the crossover circle sections, like four petals; the English North Country name for this is Cuddy's Lugs (Donkey's Ears).

Also: circles, diamonds, scotch diamonds, basketweave.

Feather Wreath Pillows

Through the ups and downs in the popularity of quilting this century, a handful of women have kept the art alive.

One of the most prominent and best known British exponents of the art is Amy Emms, who quilted the two matching pillows seen here. Born in Sunderland, England in 1904, Mrs. Emms learned the art of quilting from her mother, who ran a quilt club for many years. In order to gain a certificate as a teacher, Mrs. Emms took classes from Mary Lough, who was born in Weardale, England, in 1886 and was trained by her own mother. Mrs. Lough was probably the first person to teach formal quilting classes for an adult education project. Amy Emms subsequently became a teacher and inspired a new generation of quilters — first in Sunderland, then Weardale, and finally Tyneside. In 1983, when she eventually retired at the age of eighty, she was given a richly deserved MBE (Member of the British Empire) award.

The design used here is a traditional feather wreath, with a filling pattern of squared diamonds (smaller in the middle and larger around the outside). Feather patterns of all sorts — including wreaths, curved, and circular — are popular traditional patterns throughout Britain and the United States. The traditional way to draw feathered designs was to draw the center line of the feather and then make the curling-out lines with a small coin (a cent, for example), then link the outer curved lines inward into the central line. It is well worth practicing this for a natural and flowing effect — the central line can either be single or double like the stalk of a feather — and experimenting with making your own templates.

Don't worry if your attempts seem less than perfect. Once you start to examine antique quilts, you will discover many imperfections and hasty adjustments; without suggesting that you should make deliberate mistakes, these very trivial errors are part of the charm of handmade quilts. It is, therefore, not necessary to be a trained artist.

The backs of the covers are also quilted with a simple basketweave filling pattern. The pillows have a buttoned closing at one side. Mrs. Emms made her own thread-covered buttons, but you can either buy buttons or make fabric-covered buttons to match the cover.

This would be an excellent project for a newcomer to quilting, and you could also use other patterns in the book to design a complete set of covers.

RIGHT The design shown here is a traditional feather wreath. Although these pillows were made by a leading teacher of quilting, very few traditional quilters would have have had any formal training whatsoever.

ABILITY LEVEL:
Beginner

SIZE OF FINISHED COVER:
19 inches square

MATERIALS:
• 1⅔ yards of satin, sateen or polished cotton fabric. (This includes 1 yard, for making covered piping, with fabric cut on the cross; the piping is very thin, however, and you will need less fabric if you cut your strips straight across.)

• ⅔ yard of thin cotton fabric, for backing the quilting.

• Two pieces of batting, each 24 inches square.

• 2¼ yards of No.1 piping cord and two buttons, to match.

• 20-inch square pillow form, for a well-filled effect.

• Template (enlarge by 270%).

CUTTING
Back of cover Cut one 24-inch square piece from satin and the same from backing fabric.

Front of cover Cut one 24-inch square piece from satin and the same from backing fabric.

Button flap Cut one piece, 20 x 6 inches, from satin.

Binding Cutting on the bias, cut strips, each 1½ inches wide, to cover 2¼ yards of piping cord when joined.

MARKING
1 Take the satin cut for the pillow front and, centering it carefully, draw a 19-inch square. Draw two more squares inside the first, one of 18 inches and one of 17 inches.

2 Using the template twice, in a mirror image, draw the feathered wreath motif.

3 Finish with square-diamond filling patterns; the lines within the feathers are spaced ¾ inch apart, and the lines between the feathers and the inner square are spaced 1¼ inch apart.

4 Take the second 20-inch square of satin. Draw a 19-inch square, with an even allowance around the outside. Use a ruler to fill the marked square with the basket pattern, formed from sets of three parallel lines, each 3¼ inch long and set ⁷⁄₁₂ inch apart.

QUILTING
5 Take the marked front, batting, and backing fabric and assemble the layers (see page 17), basting thoroughly.

6 Starting with the feathers, quilt the marked design. If you are using a hoop, remember to remove the work between quilting sessions, to avoid leaving permanent marks on the fabric.

7 When you have finished the front cover, take the marked back and the second pieces of batting, and backing fabric. Assemble the layers (see page 17), basting thoroughly, and quilt the basketweave pattern.

FINISHING

8 Take the long bias strip and fold it over the piping cord; baste and stitch, close up against the cord, using the zipper foot of your sewing machine.

9 Trim the quilted front to leave a ½ inch seam allowance beyond the outer quilted square, and trim the covered piping to the same allowance.

10 With raw edges matching, pin and baste the piping around the front cover, so that the ends meet about one-third of the way along the bottom edge.

11 At the join, trim the covering to a ¼-inch overlap at each end, and unpick the stitching for about 1 inch; fold under the allowance at one end and lap this over the other, unfolded allowance. Unravel the cord ends, trimming one or two back on each side to reduce bulk, and twist them together, making a few stitches to hold them. Fold the covering back over the cord, and baste the join.

12 Stitch the piping to the front cover (along the outer quilted square), then trim the batting back close to the seamline.

13 Trim the layers of the quilted back cover to leave a ½-inch allowance beyond the outer quilted line. With right sides together, lay the button flap along the left-hand side of the back cover; pin and stitch along the outer quilted line, starting and stopping ½ inch short of the raw edge.

14 Trim the batting close to the seamline on this side. Turn under a double ¼ inch hem on the free edges of the button flap and stitch.

15 Using a double thickness of thread, and spacing them 2½ inches away from each side of the center point, make two button loops in the seam of the button flap on the right side of the fabric: take the thread from side to side several times, and then buttonhole stitch over the threads.

16 Lay the back and front covers with right sides together and stitch along the remaining three sides, again using the zipper foot and stitching close up to the piping.

17 Trim back the batting around the back cover, close to the seamline. Hand-stitch from each corner along the seamline of the open edge, leaving a 14-inch gap at the center, then turn the cover right side out.

18 To finish, stitch two buttons to the front cover, between the seam allowance and the piping, to match the loops.

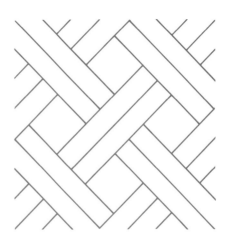

Amish Quilt

Among the most highly prized of all American antique quilts are those produced by the Amish. These Swiss Anabaptists moved to the Palatinate region of Germany and then, from about 1727, began to immigrate to Pennsylvania in small groups. Shunning the frivolity of the outside world and all non-Amish, these strictly religious communities avoided the craze for patchwork that swept 19th-century America, finding it worldly. Instead, traditional Amish quilts are restricted to a limited palette of solid fabrics, arranged in borders around a strong central image. This often took the form of a square-diamond patchwork, which symbolizes Christ, for the word diamond can also be taken to mean cornerstone (the cornerstone of the church) in German.

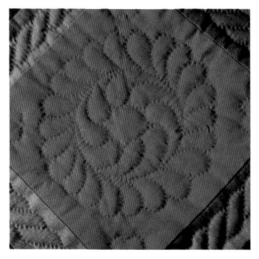

In place of detailed pieced work, Amish women executed beautiful and elaborate quilting patterns. To this day, Amish communities set themselves apart from their neighbors, and faith and religious symbolism permeate every aspect of daily life, including quilting. Although the patterns of Amish quilts are very similar to other American and British quilting patterns and motifs, they often have a particular religious connotation for the Amish. Hearts, such as those seen here, do not signify that this is a bride's quilt, but represent Christ, "the heart of man's nature," as does the rose, Christ being described as "the rose of the heart." Similarly, the tulip (popular as a quilting pattern with the Amish as it was in appliquéd form with the closely related Pennsylvania Dutch) is a form of lily, a popular flower in Christian art because of the passage: "Consider the lilies of the field, how they grow; they toil not, neither do they spin. And yet I say unto you that even Solomon in all his glory was not arrayed like one of these."

With their unusual color combinations and fine stitchery, Amish quilts have an artistic quality that makes them instantly recognizable, for no other group has achieved this perfect balance between strong color contrasts and beautiful quilting.

RIGHT AND ABOVE This small-scale Amish quilt, with its square-diamond center, features many popular Amish quilting motifs, including hearts, a central rose, and an elaborate feathered border, neatly turned at the corners.

ABILITY LEVEL:
Intermediate/Advanced

SIZE OF FINISHED QUILT:
35 inches square

MATERIALS:
• 1⅔ yards of black cotton fabric (includes fabric for backing and edging strip).

• 1 yard burgundy cotton fabric.

• ½ yard dark green cotton fabric.

• 9¾-inch square royal blue cotton fabric.

• 12 inches deep mauve cotton fabric (assumes a strip cut from fabric 45 inches wide; or use three pieces of fabric, one 16 inches square, two 6 inches square).

• 39 inches square of batting (this includes extra, to allow for shrinkage during quilting).

• Templates (enlarge by 200%).

CUTTING
Pieced front of quilt From deep burgundy fabric, cut four strips 23 x 8 inches. Deep mauve: cut four 8-inch squares and eight 3-inch squares. Green: cut four strips 19 x 3 inches and four strips 9¾ x 3 inches. Black: cut two 10¾-inch squares; cut each in half diagonally to make four triangles.

Back of cover From black fabric, cut one piece 39-inch square.

Binding From black fabric, cut two strips 1½ x 35 inches, and two strips 1½ x 36 inches.

10 At the center draw the rose, then draw a heart at each corner of the central blue square (with the point facing outward).

11 On each black triangle, draw the curled feather motif; note that at the center of each curled feather are two hearts, set point to point. Also draw a heart at the outward-facing (right-angled) corner of each black triangle, with the point set in ½ inch from the corner.

12 Draw the rope design around the green and mauve borders. Draw in the corners first to make sure these are accurate. To fit the pattern within the length, you can make minor adjustments in the spacing between strands toward the middle of each side, as necessary.

13 Finish by drawing the outer curled feather border, making sure that the feather design will be evenly spaced between the marked outer line and the border seamline. Note that where the two lines of feathering meet at each corner, there are two hearts, touching point to point, as in the black triangles.

QUILTING

14 Assemble the three layers – backing, batting, and marked top (see page 17).

15 Set the quilt in a hoop or frame, and quilt all marked lines.

16 After quilting, trim three layers back to leave the outer, burgundy border 6½ inches deep.

17 On each binding strip, fold under and then press a ¼ inch

5 As before, join a deep mauve square to each end of a green strip and repeat, then join the two unpieced strips to opposite sides of the pieced square. Join the two pieced strips to the remaining sides.

6 Join a deep mauve square to each end of a deep burgundy strip, and repeat to make two pieced strips.

7 Join the two unpieced burgundy strips to two opposite sides of the central pieced square, then join the two pieced strips to the two remaining sides. Make sure that the points of the larger and smaller corner squares meet.

8 Press top fabric and lay out on a flat surface, ready to mark the design. Start by marking central vertical and horizontal guidelines, dividing top into four quarters either by pressing or basting, as the guidelines should be removable so as not to be visible on the finished quilt.

9 Draw a line around the outer border, 6⅛ inches out from the seamline between the burgundy border and the green border.

JOINING AND MARKING

1 Taking ½ inch seam allowances throughout, join a small deep mauve square to each end of one short strip of green fabric. Repeat to make two strips the same.

2 Take the two remaining short strips of green. Join them to opposite sides of royal blue square.

3 Join the two pieced strips to the remaining sides, making sure that the corners of the larger and smaller squares meet when seamed.

4 Now join a black triangle to each side of the pieced central square. For each side, stitch along the seamline (12¾ inches long) only, leaving the seam allowance at each end free.

hem down one of the long edges and press. Then, on the two longer strips, fold under and press a ½ inch turning at each short edge.

18 Take the two shorter binding strips and attach them to two opposite sides of the quilt as follows. With raw edges and right sides matching, place the binding along the edge and stitch, taking a ¼-inch seam allowance. Bring the folded edge over to the back of the quilt and slipstitch.

19 Stitch the two remaining strips to the remaining two sides of the quilt in the same way, finishing the ends neatly.

Pink & White Star

The quilting pattern of this very handsome quilt was drawn in blue, indicating that this cover may have been marked by Elizabeth Sanderson. The design, with its large roses and trailing leafy borders, certainly bears a close resemblance to that of other quilts known to

have been marked by this remarkable woman, who lived at Fawside Green in Allendale, England, and was renowned throughout the region for the quality of her designs.

Sanderson also trained up to four apprentices at a time. Leaving school at around the age of fourteen, these young girls would be paid a small weekly sum. Jennie Liddell of Allendale, for example, was apprenticed to Elizabeth Sanderson for six years and then continued to design and make quilts until her death in the 1970s. During her apprenticeship, she was paid two shillings (10p, or approximately 15 cents) a week during her second year, and four shillings thereafter.

Elizabeth Sanderson and her apprentices also pieced and quilted patchwork designs, of which the star pattern was popular. Once an apprentice could piece and mark a star quilt such as this to Miss Sanderson's high standards, she was considered to have qualified.

LEFT AND ABOVE Possibly by Elizabeth Sanderson or one of her apprentices, the distinctive blue markings of the quilting pattern on this handsome pieced quilt are still clearly visible.

ABILITY LEVEL:
Advanced

SIZE OF FINISHED QUILT:
87½ x 97½ inches.

MATERIALS:
• 10¼ yards of white cotton fabric, for pieced top and backing.

• 5¼ yards of pink cotton fabric, for pieced top.

• 92 x 102 inches of batting (this includes extra, to allow for shrinkage during the quilting process).

• Templates for quilting and pieced shapes (page 124; enlarge by 250%).

CUTTING
NOTE: Throughout this project, "**i**" refers to the top and bottom border strips, and "**ii**" refers to the side border strips.

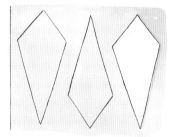

Central star When cutting out the pieces for the central star, use the templates to mark the shapes on the wrong side of the fabric, using a well-sharpened pencil, and leaving a space of at least ½ inch between marked shapes. Cut out, adding a ¼ inch seam allowance around each marked shape. From the white fabric, using template A, cut out the central 8-point star.

Using templates C (triangles) and D (corners), cut four shapes of each type (make sure that the edges that will lie along the outer square, adjacent to the first, white border, are cut along the grainlines). From the pink fabric, using template B, cut out eight shapes (the outer points of the star).

Border 1 From the white fabric, cut two strips (**i**) 3 x 34½ inches, and two strips (**ii**) 3 x 39½ inches.

Border 2 From the pink fabric, cut two strips (**i**) 5 x 39½ inches, and two strips (**ii**) 5 x 47½ inches.

Border 3 From the white fabric, cut two strips (**i**) 7½ x 47½ inches, and two strips (**ii**) 5¼ x 60½ inches.

Border 4 From the pink fabric, cut two strips (**i**) 5 x 56 inches, and two strips (**ii**) 5 x 68½ inches.

Border 5 From the white fabric, cut two strips (**i**) 7½ x 64 inches, and two strips (**ii**) 5¼ x 81½ inches.

Border 6 From the pink fabric, cut two strips (**i**) 11 x 72½ inches, and two strips (**ii**) 10½ x 81½ inches. From the white fabric, cut four corner pieces 11 x 10½ inches.

Back of cover From the white fabric, cut two pieces 25 x 101½ inches, and one piece 43½ x 101½ inches.

PIECING
1 The central patchwork star shape can be stitched either by hand or by machine. The marked lines are seam-

lines, and stitching should not run beyond these lines into the seam allowance, which is ¼ in. Backstitch at the beginning and end of each seam-

line. Start by setting a pink star point into one of the angles of the central white star. Starting at the inner corner, pin the pink piece along one side of the angle, taking care to match seamlines and pinning to the outside

edge. Stitch from the inner corner to the outer edge (do not stitch beyond the marked lines).

2 Next, pin and stitch along the other side, again working from the inner corner outward. At the inner corner, take a notch from the seam allowance of the pink piece – as shown – to remove excess fabric. To finish, press the seam allowances to the pink side.

3 Repeat this, until all eight points of the pink star have been joined to the central white star.

4 Now, one by one, attach the corner pieces (D) to the central shape, again piecing the angled seams from the inner corner outward and stitching along seamlines only. Press the seams open, where necessary cutting across the seam allowance at the corners to remove excess fabric.

5 Join in the C triangles. As each of these is joined, the base of the triangle should run on a straight line with the adjacent edges of the corner pieces, so you finish with a large square shape.

6 Attach the two short border 1 strips (**i**) to two opposite sides – now the top and bottom – of the pieced star, and attach the remaining border 1 strips to the two remaining sides.

7 The central pieced section is now complete. For all subsequent seams, take a seam allowance of ½ inch.

Always attaching the top and bottom strips (**i**) first, join on borders 2, 3, 4, and 5 in the same way as border 1.

8 Join a white corner piece to each end of each of the long border 6 strips (**ii**). Join the short strips to the top and bottom of the pieced cover, and then join the pieced side strips.

MARKING

9 To mark the pattern, use either a blue pencil, like that used for marking the original quilt, or an unobtrusive marker of your choice. Begin by drawing in the straight grid lines. At the central star, draw lines at each side of the seamlines, ⅜ inch away from the seams where the pink rays meet the central star and where they meet the white C and D patches.

10 Spacing the lines an equal distance from the raw edge on all sides, draw a rectangle measuring 86½ x 96½ inches. This marks the outer edge of the quilting pattern, and leaves a width of 8 inches between the marked quilting line and the inner seamline on both the top and bottom border 6 strips, and 7½ inches on the side strips.

11 Outline borders 1, 3, and 5 (white) by drawing straight lines

echoing the seamlines between these and the adjacent (pink) borders 2, 2 and 4, and 4 and 6; the lines are spaced ¼ inch from the seamlines, on the white border side only. When drawing the lines around border 1, note that they intersect at the corners and cross, finishing at the far side of the pink border 2 strips.

12 At the center of the quilt, draw a large rose contained within a circle (with a diameter of 7 inches). Repeat this same motif at the four outer corners within an additional circle of 7¾ inches, containing the roses within the corner seamlines and the outer quilting line.

13 The rays of the central white star are echoed by a line of contour quilting, ⅜ inch in from the seamline. Now draw smaller rays, with sides 1½ inches long, from the edge of the outer circle around the rose.

14 Within the quilting outline of each pink ray of the star, draw the rose and stem motif.

15 Then fill the white area surrounding the star, between the marked contour quilting lines, with square diamonds, setting the lines 1¼ inches apart.

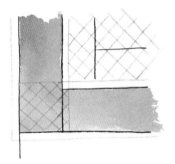

16 Fill the corners of border 2, in the areas between the outer seamlines and the crossed quilting lines of border 1, with square-diamonds, setting the lines 1 inch apart. Starting from the center of each border strip and working outward, fill each border

2 strip with the smaller, double-strand twist.

17 Repeat this pattern, including the square-diamond corners, on border 4.

18 The white borders 3 and 5 are filled with the trailing stems. In each case, start by drawing a three-leaved motif at each corner.

19 The stems trail out along the borders from the spaces between the leaves, meeting at the center, as shown. These stems, with their leafy shapes and scrolls contained within the marked outer quilting lines, were

drawn freehand on the original quilt. To achieve the same free-flowing effect, it would be best to draw them freehand. If you do not wish to risk this, draw them first on paper (butcher's paper would be ideal). Outline your sketches in black marker pen to make them stand out, then use one of the methods given on page 61 to transfer them to the fabric borders.

20 At the outer border (6), starting from the center of each border strip and working out to the corner in each direction, draw the larger, four-strand twist. The twists run up to the outer circles surrounding the corner roses.

QUILTING

21 Then, taking ½ inch seam allowances, join the three lengths cut for the back, setting the wide piece in the middle. Press both seams open.

22 Assemble the three layers — backing, batting, and marked top (see page 17).

23 Quilt all marked lines, including the outer marked line.

24 When you have finished quilting, trim the batting back to within a scant ½ inch of the outer quilted line.

25 Trim the top and backing fabrics to within ½ inch of the batting. Then bring the top fabric over the edge of

the batting, and turn under the edge of the backing fabric to meet it. Pin and baste.

26 Topstitch the front and back together neatly, stitching close to the folded edges.

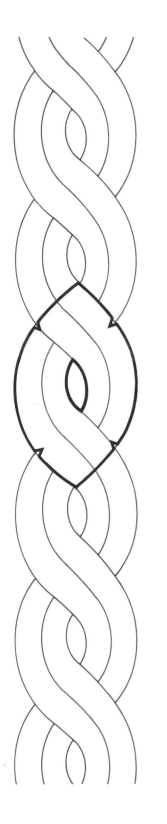

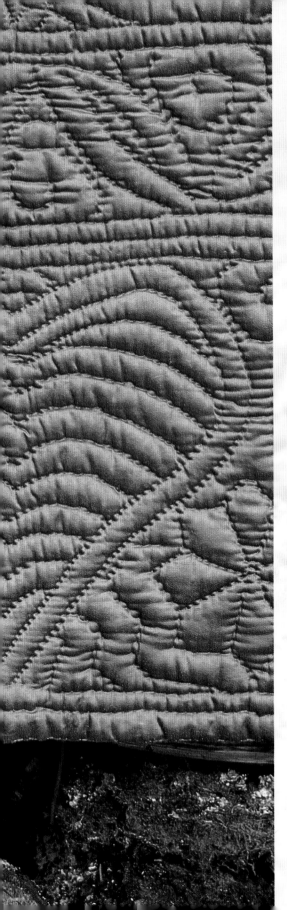

Wholecloth Quilting

With wholecloth quilting, the emphasis is on the pattern and the quality of the stitching, with no distractions from patches and patterns. It was traditionally the showcase of the quilter's art and skill. It is therefore no coincidence that a large number have survived in pristine condition, compared with the number of strippies that show marks, tears, and worn patches from years of washing and use. Quilted masterpieces, such as the ones illustrated in this section of the book, were only brought out on very special occasions.

Welsh Quilt

This heavily sculptured Welsh quilt, with its rich coloring, is made from sateen, in what one Welsh quilter referred to as "the grandest colors."

Strong, dark colors were particularly favored in Wales for wedding quilts, and the outer border of large hearts is another indication that this may indeed have been a wedding quilt. The women who designed such quilts were often itinerant, traveling from farm to farm in country areas. They would stay at each dwelling long enough to replenish the stock of everyday quilts required not only for the farmer and his

family, but also for the hired help and, where needed, to make *cwiltiau stafell*, or dowry quilts.

The spiral "Welsh rose" or "snail creep" motif, repeated in the borders and corners of the central area, is found in many Welsh quilts, and is reminiscent of early Celtic jewelry and sculpture, and the elaborate carvings found on love spoons.

Leaf designs of one form or another were also very popular on Welsh quilts, though they are equally to be found on many English quilts. Welsh designs have been referred to as more geometric and less free-flowing than English designs – and the heavily sculptured design seen here certainly fits this image.

RIGHT AND ABOVE This early 20th-century Welsh quilt is probably a wedding quilt; it is more thickly padded than many quilts, which adds to the relief effect of the design, and it is reversible – green on one side and rust on the other.

ABILITY LEVEL:
Advanced

SIZE OF FINISHED QUILT:
68 x 81½ inches

MATERIALS
• 5 yards of rust cotton sateen fabric and the same of rich moss green cotton sateen, one for the top and the other for the backing (reverse side).

• 72 x 85½ inches of batting (includes extra, to allow for shrinkage during quilting).

• Templates (enlarge by 250%).

CUTTING
Front of cover Green fabric – one piece 29½ x 85½ inches, and one 15 x 85½ inches.

Back of cover Rust fabric – one piece 29½ x 85½ inches, and one 143½ x 85½ inches.

JOINING AND MARKING
1 First assemble the pieces for the front: taking ½ inch seam allowances, join the two lengths cut for the (green) top and then press the seam open.

2 Join the (rust) back in the same way.

3 Press the top fabric and lay it out on a flat surface. Mark central vertical and horizontal guidelines, dividing the top into four quarters. Do this by pressing or basting, as the guidelines should be easily removable, so as not to be visible on the finished quilt.

4 To mark the quilting design, first draw the outer limit of the quilted border: a rectangle 66½ x 80 inches, making sure that opposite sides are equally spaced from the center. (To check, fold the rectangle diagonally each way – the diagonals should be the same length and cross at the marked center.) Within this, mark a second rectangle, an even ¾ inch in from the first.

5 Measure in 11 inches on all sides, and mark a rectangle 43 x 56½ inches; measure in a further ½ inch on all sides and mark a rectangle, and again a further ½ inch, to mark the third of the rectangles separating

the inner and outer borders (41 x 54½ inches).

6 From the innermost rectangle, measure in 4½ inches at the top and bottom, and draw a line across, touching the rectangle on each side, then draw a second line at the top and bottom, ½ inch in from the previous

line. Measure in 4½ inches from each side and again draw two lines, intersecting the top and bottom lines at the corners. This completes the second, inner border.

7 Measure in a further 8¼ inches from the top and bottom of the second border, and draw two lines, ½ inch apart, meeting the inner border lines at the sides, and leaving a rectangle 31 x 27 inches at the center.

8 Draw in the central motifs — four pairs of leaves, facing outward, with a rose between each pair, and Welsh rose spirals at the corners; note that bottoms of the pairs of leaves that face out to the top and bottom edges of the quilt meet at the middle, and the sideways-pointing leaves fit in the gaps.

9 Next, draw the twist-edged fan borders above and below the central section. If you examine the picture of the original, you will see that the maker had some trouble arranging the fans on one of the strips, and finished with four and a bit. The trick is to overlap the first shape by slightly more than the subsequent fans.

10 Draw the inner border of small leaves; these are arranged in a zigzag pattern, with spirals filling the spaces above and below, and large spirals at each corner. (On the longer, side edges, the leaves do not quite touch the containing lines of the border, but this does not show when they have been quilted.)

11 Finish with the outer border: draw a pair of leaves at each corner, then the hearts — six at the top and bottom and seven down each long side.

Put roses between the hearts around the outer edge, and spirals to fill the spaces at the inner edge. Note that each rose has two curved lines on each side, between the rose and the edge of the heart.

QUILTING

12 Assemble three layers: backing, batting, and marked top (page 17).

13 Quilt all marked lines, including the outer marked line. When quilting the Welsh rose spirals, you can spiral from the inside out; if you have drawn fairly close-set spirals, however, and stitch from the outside in, you can produce a small peak at the center of the rose.

14 When you have finished quilting, trim the batting back to within a scant ¾ inch of the outer quilted line.

15 Trim the top and backing fabrics to within ½ inch of the batting, then bring the top fabric over the edge of the batting, and turn under the edge of the backing fabric to meet it. Pin and baste.

16 Topstitch the front and back neatly together, stitching as close as you can to the folded edges.

Bordered White Quilt

This white wholecloth quilt features a strongly bordered design. It has a deep outer border which has been quilted in a twist pattern, and this is echoed by an inner border of running feathers. The central motif has a large feathered circle, with a rose at the center and large leaves around the inside. These large leafy outlines were sometimes called flat-irons, because they could be made by drawing around the sides and pointed end of two old-fashioned flat-irons, placed back to back. The resulting shape can be filled with a wide variety of designs, including roses with stems and leaves.

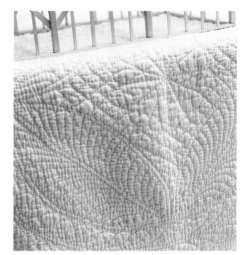

The twist design, made with an oval template, can also be found with numerous fillings. This particular oval is so plump that the central eye usually found in twist patterns has been criss-crossed. Other popular variations include the trail, in which only one side of the twist is lined; the lined and feathered twist, one side of which is lined, interlinking with a second, feathered side; and the Weardale chain, in which the linked ovals are filled with roses and chevrons. It is possible to turn corners with a twist pattern by looping the outer edge around the corner in a deep curve, and shortening the other, inner side of the twist, but here the quilter has dealt with the problem by setting a large fan at each corner.

LEFT AND ABOVE A common difficulty when making a large quilt such as this is to keep it clean during the prolonged quilting process. Areas of the quilt not being worked on should be covered up with a clean sheet.

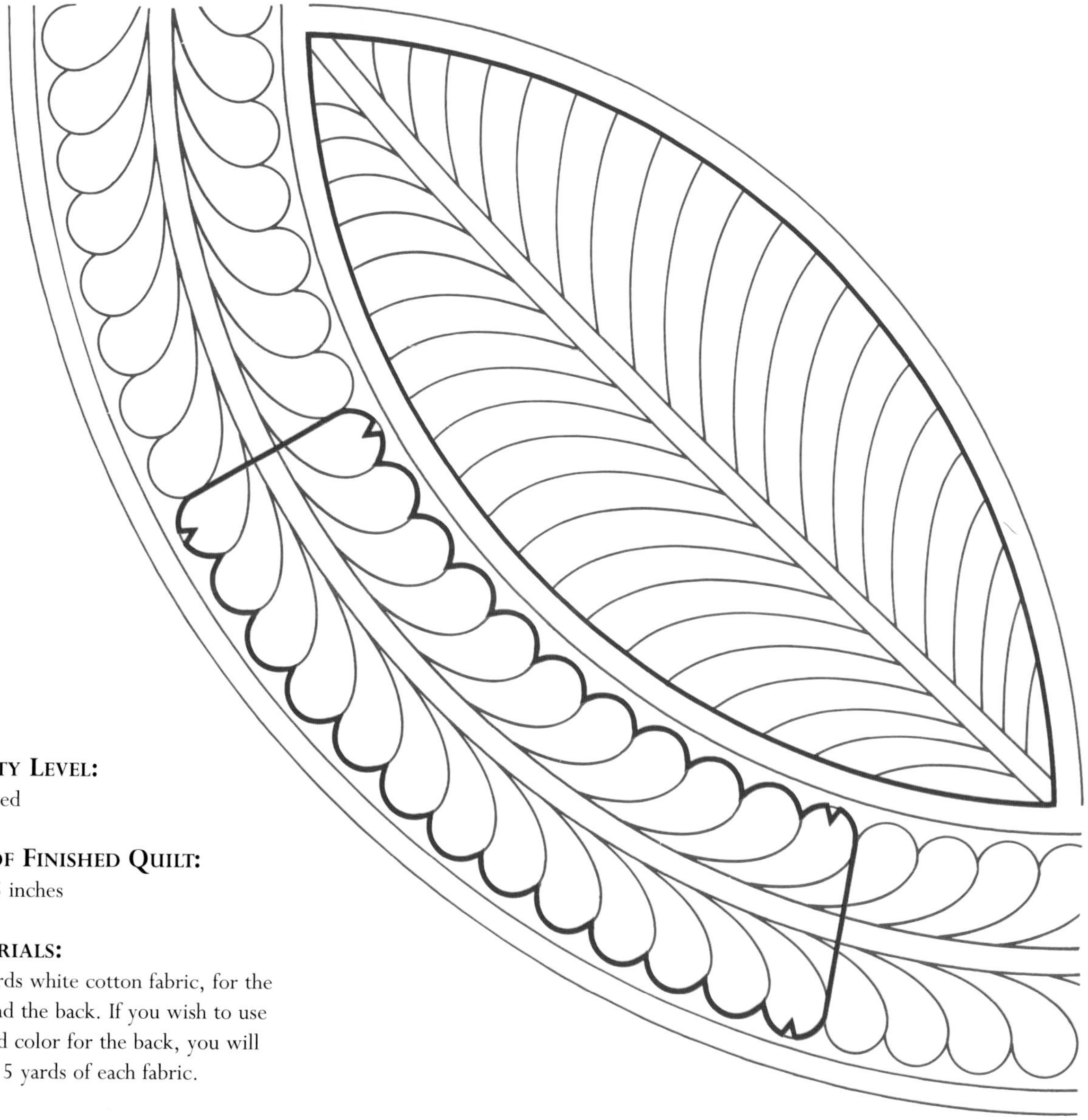

ABILITY LEVEL:
Advanced

SIZE OF FINISHED QUILT:
71 x 85 inches

MATERIALS:
• 10 yards white cotton fabric, for the front and the back. If you wish to use a second color for the back, you will require 5 yards of each fabric.

• 75 x 89 inches of batting (includes extra, to allow for shrinkage during quilting).

• Templates for quilting.

CUTTING

Front of cover From white fabric, cut two pieces 16½ x 89 inches, and one piece 44 x 89 inches.

Back of cover From white fabric, cut two pieces 17½ x 89 inches, and one piece 42 x 89 inches.

JOINING AND MARKING

1 First assemble the pieces for the front. Taking ½ inch seam allowances, join the three lengths cut for the top, setting the wide piece in the middle. Press both seams open.

2 Join the three pieces cut for the back in the same way.

3 Press the top fabric and lay it out carefully on a flat surface, (see page 17), ready to mark the design. Start by marking central vertical and horizontal guidelines, dividing the top into four quarters. Do this either by pressing or basting, as the guidelines should be easily removable so that they will not be visible on the finished quilt.

4 To mark the quilting design, first draw the outer limit of the quilted border: a rectangle measuring 70 x 84 inches, making sure that opposite sides are equally spaced from the center. (To check, fold the rectangle diagonally each way; the diagonals should be the same length and cross at the marked center.) Within this, mark a second rectangle ½ inch in from the first on all sides.

5 Measure in 8 inches on all sides, and mark a rectangle, then measure in a further ½ inch and mark another rectangle. This completes the lines enclosing the border pattern.

6 From the marked center of the quilt, draw two circles, one with a radius of 15⅜ inches, and one with a radius of 15 inches. Still from the center, draw another two circles, one

with a radius of 11⅜ inches, and one with a radius of 11 inches. This completes the main dividing lines of the quilt.

7 Again from the center, draw two more circles – one should have a radius of 13⅜ inches and the other a radius of 13 inches. These form the central lines of the feather circlet. To mark in the rest of the circlet, you should either use a template or draw in the outer shaping of the feathers by hand in the traditional manner, using a suitable coin (a coin with a diameter of about ½ inch appears to have been used here). For a well-shaped feather circlet, the lines should curve gracefully into the central stem.

8 Using the rose template, draw a rose at the center of the quilt, and then use the large leaf template to

surround this central rose with four leaves.

9 Draw eight more large roses, each ½ inch beyond the outer circle, using the marked central guidelines to position the roses around the circle.

10 Within the inner border frame, and spaced ⅛ inch away from it at the closest point, draw running feathers along the top and bottom of the quilt.

11 Draw a rose at each corner, just below the running feathers at the top, and just above those at the bottom. Then draw running feathers down each side, from rose to rose.

12 Within the border, draw a fan at each corner then, in each case starting from the center and working out

evenly to the fan at each corner, draw the twist pattern along the top and bottom and side borders.

13 To finish, draw the square-diamond filling pattern in the central area, within the inner border frame, spacing the lines 1 inch apart.

QUILTING

14 Assemble the three layers – backing, batting, and marked top.

15 Quilt all marked lines, including the outer marked line. When quilting the twist, use a separate needle for each line of the twist, working a short length of one line, and then moving on to the next, and completing a section at a time.

16 After you have finished the quilting, you should trim the batting to extend just ¼ inch beyond the outer quilted line.

17 Trim the top and backing fabrics to within 1 inch of the quilted line, and finish with a folded edge.

Fan Border Quilt

This very handsome reversible quilt – bright yellow sateen on one side and a light, almost apple, green on the other – is beautifully designed and carefully stitched. Judging by its luxurious appearance, it may well have been made in England for sale in the London market, under the auspices of either the Rural Industries Bureau (RIB) or the Northern Industries Workroom Clubs, which had two centers, one in Barnard Castle and the other in Langley Moor.

The borders of the other wholecloth quilts in this section are separated from the central design by a clear dividing framework, but here the square-diamond filling pattern links the fans of the border

with the centerpiece, somewhat in the Sanderson/Gardiner style. Fans are a popular quilting motif, either repeated, as in this case, or as a useful corner pattern. Like certain other quilting patterns, such as flower baskets or tulips, they are also a popular patchwork/appliqué motif, with each spoke of the pattern known as Grandmother's Fan being made

from a different fabric, and then the whole applied to a background square. The shapes on each side of these fans are repeated in a larger format at the center of the quilt. Apart from this, the central design is similar to that of the quilt on page 110, and you could easily switch elements from one to the other, if you choose.

RIGHT AND ABOVE Made in the years between the two world wars, this brightly colored quilt, with its border of fans and curling decorative motifs, is of a particularly high standard.

ABILITY LEVEL:
Advanced

SIZE OF FINISHED QUILT:
82 x 91½ inches

MATERIALS:
• 5⅛ yards of bright yellow sateen or satin fabric, for top of quilt.

• 8 yards of light green sateen or satin fabric, for backing.

• 86 x 95½ inches of batting (this includes extra, to allow for shrinkage during quilting).

• Templates (enlarge by 250%). Note: the quantity given for the

backing assumes the fabric is 45 inches wide and cut to avoid matching seams at the front and back of the quilt, which would make quilting across seamlines difficult. If you use a wider fabric, you will require only twice the length of the quilt, plus 8 inches.

CUTTING
Front of cover From yellow fabric, cut two pieces 22 x 95½ inches, and one piece 44 x 95½ inches.

Back of cover From light green fabric, cut two pieces 24 x 95½ inches, and one piece 40 x 95½ inches.

JOINING AND MARKING

1 First assemble the pieces for the front. Taking ½-inch seam allowances, join three lengths cut for the (yellow) top, with the wide piece in the middle. Press both seams open.

2 Join (green) back in the same way.

3 Press the top fabric and lay it out carefully on a flat surface (see page 17), ready to mark the design. Start by marking central vertical and horizontal guidelines, dividing the top into four quarters. Do this either by pressing or basting, as the guidelines should be easily removable so that they will not be visible on the finished quilt.

4 To mark the quilting design, first draw a rectangle measuring 80½ x 90 inches, making sure that opposite sides are an equal distance from the center. This rectangle will be the outer quilted line and will be ¼ inch from the folded edge of the quilt.

5 Draw in the central large rose, then the eight straight feathers that are evenly spaced around the rose

(use the marked guidelines to position these). Fill the spaces between feathers with small curlicues (these can easily be drawn freehand).

6 Next, draw the flat-iron shapes that extend from the tip of each straight feather, with a gap of ¼ inch between the tip of the feather and the end of the flat-iron. Draw a small rose inside each end of the flat iron, then fill the space between with square-diamond filling, as shown, spacing the lines ¾ inch apart. Leaving a space of ⅜ inch, set another large rose at the outer tip of each flat iron.

7 Extending from the top section of each straight feather and the tip of the adjacent flat iron, draw a large "finger" shape. From each of these, draw two small fronds, echoing the curve of the flat-iron shapes at each side. Between these draw a large pineapple-top motif, with a small rose set at the tip.

8 For the fan border, start at the corners. At each corner, measure in 3 inches from the outer marked quilting line at each side and draw a line 8 inches long. The intersection between the two lines marks the placement of the corner fan. Then draw a fan at each corner.

9 Draw the remaining border fans, six along each long side and five along each short side (not counting corner fans). At the left side of each fan draw a smaller "finger" motif curling upward, and to the right draw a medium-sized "finger" motif curling downward.

10 Complete the fan border by drawing a right-angled grid of lines at the

corners, setting the lines 1 inch apart, and running from the finger motifs to the outer quilting line.

11 Fill the remaining area between the central design and the fans with square-diamond filling, spacing the lines 1 inch apart.

QUILTING
12 Assemble the three layers – backing, batting, and marked top.

13 Quilt all marked lines, including the outer marked line.

14 When you have finished quilting, trim the batting back to within ½ inch of the outer quilted line.

15 Trim the top and backing fabrics to within ½ inch of the batting, then bring the top fabric over the edge of the batting, and turn in the edge of the backing fabric to meet it. Pin and baste.

16 Topstitch the folded edges of the front and back together neatly, stitching close to the fold.

Yellow Quilt

In the 19th century, quilts were often filled with unrefined cotton, and the seeds can be seen in this highly decorative antique French quilt when held against the light. There are also hard little bumps in the padding, where the cotton filling has gathered in lumps over the years, distorting the quilting pattern in places. Today, we are lucky to have available top-quality polyester and other prepared battings, which hold their shape well and are easier to stitch. There is no reason why reproducing an attractive pattern of this type should include recreating the problems faced by the original maker!

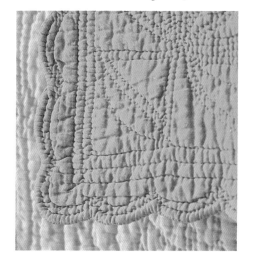

The quilting pattern is formed largely from two repeated leaf shapes — a laurel leaf circle at the center, and a variety of floral and leafy patterns arranged around the border; the two being linked by a triple-lined version of the familiar square-diamond filling. The delicate scalloped edging adds an unusual and very charming touch to this pretty quilt, serving to soften the geometric lines.

The center of the quilt contains three circles with three leaves in the middle, and the square template turned on its axis and repeated three times; it is perhaps the least successful part of this otherwise effective design. If you prefer, you might fill this area with a rose, or perhaps a motif of your own.

RIGHT AND ABOVE Smaller than many quilts, this was probably made for the top of a double bed, allowing for a display of lacy or embroidered pillows and sheets. The same bright yellow was used for both the back and front.

ABILITY LEVEL:
Intermediate

SIZE OF FINISHED QUILT:
59 x 66½ inches

MATERIALS:
• 6 yards of bright yellow cotton fabric, for the top and the backing; if you wish to have a contrasting backing, you will need 4 yards each of the top fabric and the backing.

• 63 x 70½ inches of batting (this includes extra, to allow for shrinkage during quilting and for shaping the scalloped edge; to avoid having problems with this, use a relatively thin batting).

• Templates (enlarge by 250%); and a 3¾ inch square template.

CUTTING
Front and back of cover Cut two pieces 44 x 70½ inches, and two pieces 20 x 70½ inches, all from yellow fabric.

JOINING AND MARKING
1 First assemble the pieces for the front and back. Taking ½-inch seam allowances, join one wide piece to one narrower piece down one long edge. Then press the seams open and repeat this process with the remaining two pieces.

2 Press the top fabric and lay it out carefully on a flat surface (see page 17). Start by marking central vertical and horizontal guidelines, dividing the top into four quarters. Do this either by pressing or basting, as the guidelines should be easily removable so that they will not be visible on the finished quilt.

3 First mark the outer limit of the border, not including the scalloped edge – a rectangle measuring 56½ x 64 inches – making sure that opposite sides are equally spaced from the center. (To check, fold the rectangle diagonally each way – the diagonals should be the same length and cross at the marked center.) Within this, mark two more rectangles, spaced ⅛ inch apart, to make three parallel lines on all edges.

4 Leave a gap of 5½ inches, then draw another border rectangle, and then

two more, again spaced ⅛ inch apart (the outermost rectangle should be 6⅝ inches from the innermost one).

5 Next, mark the central circular design, which is contained within three sets of circles. The easiest way to draw these would be to use ordinary household objects (as quilters did in olden times), such as wineglasses, or cups, saucers and plates. You will probably find the sizes you need, see steps 6, 7, and 8, without much difficulty.

If not, you can easily make templates from thin cardboard, using a pair of compasses.

6 The first, innermost circle has a diameter of 2¼ inches, and is echoed by two more circles, one with a diameter of 3¼ inches, and the next with a diameter of 3¾ inches. Mark these circles then, using the leaf template, fill the innermost circle with the leaf design, as shown.

7 The next set, which consists of four circles radiating from the center of the quilt, starts with a circle with a diameter of 5½ inches, followed by circles measuring 6 inches, 6½ inches and 7 inches in diameter. Mark these circles, then use the 3¾ inch square template to mark three squares, enclosing the first, innermost set of circles, and turning the template through 60° each time for the second and third squares.

8 The next set consists of three circles measuring 12 inches, 12½ inches and 13 inches in diameter. Mark these circles, then lightly mark another circle, 9½ inches diameter, between the last two sets of circles. Again, using the leaf template, draw pairs of leaves with short stalks leading into the 9½ inch circle, turning it into a wreath of leaves.

9 Now mark the border, starting from the center of each side and working outward toward the corners. Using the 3¾ inch square template, draw five diamond shapes between the inner and outer border lines on each side of the quilt (note that the points do not touch the lines). Within each square-diamond, draw a second square,

spaced ⅛ inch from the outer square.
Fill with the appropriate designs;
each side of the quilt has one design in
the center of the border, with two
pairs of matching squares at each side.
The triangular spaces between squares
are filled with a design formed by
three leaves.

10 Draw in the corner designs within
the border and then, using the larger
leaf template, mark the leafy stems
that project from the corners to meet
the central diamond.

11 Having completed the border and
center, draw in the remaining corner
designs which project into the filling
pattern – one large leaf framed by
two stems of smaller leaves. (I suspect
that the curved outer edge of this
design was formed by drawing around
the side of a small meat dish, which
would save making a template!)

12 Draw the triple-lined square-
diamond pattern, formed by sets of
three lines, each spaced ⅜ inches
apart, with 2 inches between each set.
If this is your first large-scale project,
take care: filler patterns seem easy but
in fact they can cause great problems,
because the human eye automatically
detects slight linear irregularities.

13 Finally, draw the scalloped edge.
The outermost curve of each scallop
lies 1¼ inches from the outer border
line. Start from the center of each
side and work out toward the corner.
At each corner, join the two rows of
scallops with a neat curve.

QUILTING

14 Assemble the three layers (see
page 17) – backing, batting, and
marked top – making sure that the

seam at the back runs down the opposite side to the seam at the front, to
avoid having to stitch through too
many layers.

15 Quilt all marked lines, with the
exception of the outer scalloped line
(quilt the inner lines of scallops).

16 When you have finished quilting,
trim the batting back to within a scant
¼ inch of the scalloped quilted line
(not the outer, unquilted line).

17 Trim the top and backing fabrics to
within ⅛ inch of the marked,
unquilted outer edge, then bring the
top fabric over the edge of the
batting, and turn in the edge of the
backing fabric to meet it. Pin and
baste; note that you will have to cut
almost up to the marked seamline at
the inner point of the scallops, in
order to turn the allowance under.

18 Slipstitch the folded edges neatly
and invisibly along the scalloped edge,
taking care to secure inner corners.
You will need patience to do this
when you are so near the end, but the
result will be worth the effort!

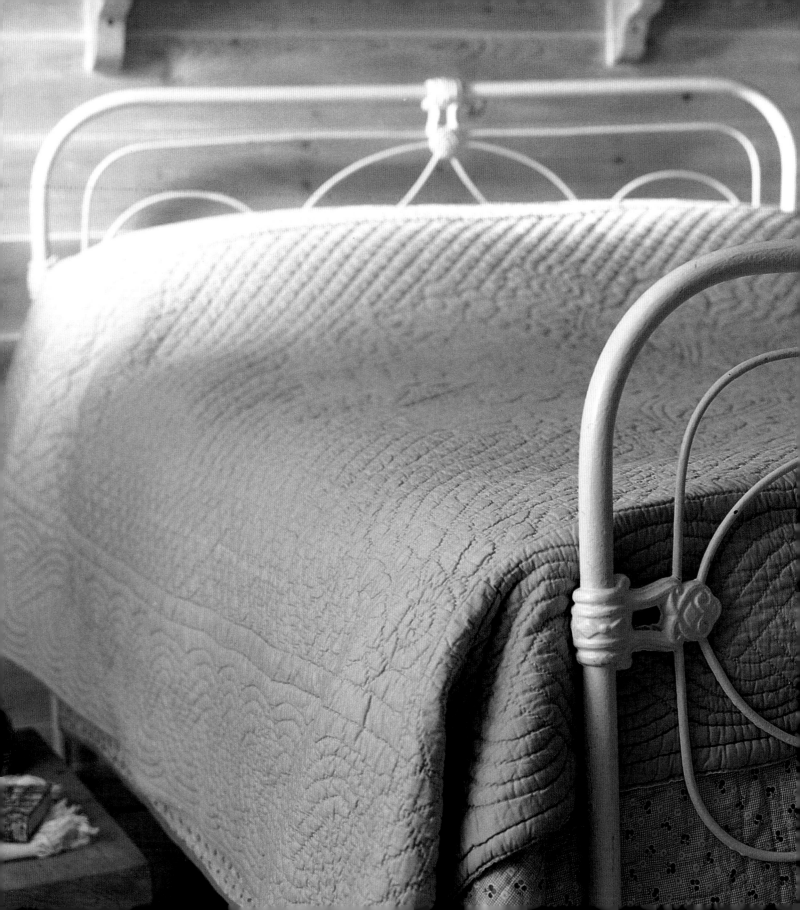

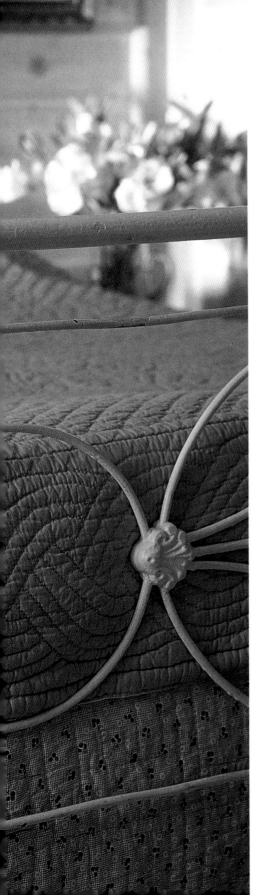

Roses and Feathers

This attractive and beautifully stitched English North Country quilt features a combination of design styles. The central design, which extends freely out into the background filling (as do the inner corners, with their leafy stems and roses) is in the free-flowing style of George Gardiner and Elizabeth Sanderson. However, the plaited border, contained within double lines and with a square-diamond filling at the four corners, contrasts with the central pattern.

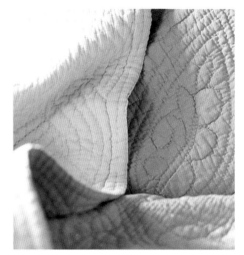

The result is a halfway house between the two different styles. It seems likely, however, that this quilt could have been made by one of the quilt "clubs" that flourished in England around the turn of the century and up until the World War 1. The women who ran these clubs, usually because they had become the breadwinner through the death, industrial injury, or unemployment of their husbands, made only a small weekly profit, with about two-thirds of the money paid for a quilt going to the cost of materials. There was no time to quilt elaborate borders in the Gardiner style, and the central designs were simplified. Blue was a favorite color for wholecloth quilts, as were apple-green, and white and off-white. This particular quilt is reversible – blue on one side, and white the other.

LEFT AND ABOVE This beautifully stitched quilt from the north of England includes a wide variety of design styles. The central design of leafy stems and roses is in the style of Gardiner and Sanderson.

ABILITY LEVEL: Advanced

SIZE OF FINISHED COVER:
81 x 87 inches

MATERIALS:
• 5¼ yards of white cotton fabric, for the backing.

• 85 x 91 inches of batting (this includes extra, allowing for shrinkage during quilting).

• Templates (enlarge by 250%).

CUTTING
Front of cover From blue fabric, cut two pieces 21½ x 91 inches, and one 44 x 91 inches.

Back of cover From white fabric, cut two pieces 22½ x 91 inches, and one 42 x 91 inches.

JOINING AND MARKING
1 First assemble the pieces for the front: taking ½ inch seam allowances, join the three lengths cut for the (blue) top, setting the wide piece in the middle. Press both seams open.

2 Join (white) back in the same way.

3 Press the top fabric and lay it out carefully on a flat surface (see page 17), ready to mark the design. Start by marking central vertical and horizontal guidelines, dividing the top into four quarters. Do this either by pressing or basting, as the guidelines should be easily removable, so that they will not be visible on the finished quilt.

4 To mark the quilting design, first draw the outer limit of the quilted border: a rectangle 79 x 85 inches, making sure that opposite sides are equally spaced from the center. (To check, fold the rectangle diagonally each way – the diagonals should be the same length and cross at the

marked center.) Within this, mark a second rectangle, an even 1 inch in from the first.

5 Measure in 7¾ inches on all sides, and mark lines running across from marked edge to marked edge; measure in a further 1 inch on all sides and mark a rectangle.

6 Draw in the central large rose, then the eight straight feathers that are evenly spaced around the rose (use the guidelines to position these).

Between each pair of straight feathers, draw a circle ¾ inch in diameter.

7 Next, draw the flat-iron shapes that extend from the tip of each straight feather. Leaving a space of ½ inch, set another large rose at the outer tip of each flat-iron.

8 Between each pair of straight feathers, put a small circle, then in each space between a pair of feathers and flat-irons, draw a medium rose and then a circle-and-frond, leaving a

gap of ½ inch between the rose and the circled end of the frond. Finish by drawing the pairs of leafy trails that start between each rose and flat-iron tip, and almost touch at the tip of each circle-and-frond shape.

9 Draw the inner corner motifs. These start with a triple circle (3¼ inches, 1¼ inches, and ½ inch in diameter), set 1 inch from each side of the inner marked border, with three stems extending from each, each tipped with a small rose.

10 Draw the plaited design along each border, always starting at the center of a border strip to finish with an equal amount of plaiting at corresponding corners.

11 Then fill each of the corner squares of the border with square-diamond filling, spacing the lines 1 inch apart; fill in the central area of the quilt around the motifs with a square-diamond filling again, spacing the lines 1⅛ inches apart.

QUILTING

12 Assemble the three layers — backing, batting, and marked top.

13 Quilt all marked lines, including the outer marked line.

14 When you have finished quilting, trim the batting back to within a scant 1 inch of the outer quilted line.

15 Trim the top and backing fabrics to within ½ inch of the batting, then bring the top fabric over the edge of

the batting, and turn under the edge of the backing fabric to meet it. Pin and baste.

16 Topstitch the front and back neatly together — stitching close to the folded edges.

Child's Play Quilt

This is a highly eccentric, yet extremely attractive quilt. The quilting design follows none of the usual rules and cannot be ascribed to any particular region. Judging from the cotton filling, and from the general wear and tear, it is old, but without specific knowledge it is virtually impossible to put an accurate date to it. The design, however, is reminiscent of some 1920s and 1930s fabrics, so it could well date from that era.

Essentially, the overall pattern resembles a giant doodle, where order struggles against chaos. The borders don't really relate to each

other and, although the shapes echo each other from quarter to quarter, they haven't been positioned very accurately – they are very crowded, with no background filler patterns to provide the usual contrast between raised and closely quilted areas. This said, the end result has a naive charm all of its own: it may not be orthodox, but it is fun.

Perhaps, quite literally, a child got hold of some of her mother's quilting templates, played around with them, and was then taught how to make her own quilt. It would certainly be one way of introducing a child to the art of quilting. With this in mind, and because of the nature of the design, the method suggested for planning and marking this quilt is slightly unusual.

RIGHT AND ABOVE There are several ways of displaying an antique quilt such as this. One very simple way is to blindstitch a fabric channel to the back of the quilt and place a pole through it.

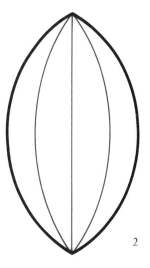

1

2

3

ABILITY LEVEL:
Beginner/Intermediate

SIZE OF FINISHED COVER:
78½ x 80 inches

MATERIALS:
• 14 yards of pink cotton fabric, for the top and the backing; if you wish to have a contrasting backing, you will need 7 yards each of the top fabric and the backing. (Note: as with all quantities in this book, this assumes a width of 45 inches; you could, however, use the same length of fabric 36 inches wide.)

• 82½ x 84 inches of batting (this includes extra, to allow for shrinkage during quilting).

• Templates for quilting (enlarge by 250%). Photocopies of quilting templates, see steps 7–10, below.

CUTTING
Front of cover Three lengths of pink fabric; one being 29 x 84 inches, and two being 27¾ x 84 inches.

Back of cover Three lengths of pink fabric – one being 27 x 84 inches, and two being 28¾ x 84 inches.

JOINING AND MARKING
1 First assemble the pieces for the front: taking ½ inch seam allowances, join the three lengths cut for the front. Press both seams open.

2 Join the pieces cut for the back in the same way.

3 Press the top fabric and lay it out

on a flat surface, ready to mark the design. Start by marking central horizontal and vertical guidelines, dividing the top into four quarters. Do this either by pressing or by basting, as these marks will not be quilted and should be easily removable.

4 To mark the quilting design, first mark the outer limit of the quilted border – a rectangle measuring

77 x 78½ inches (you must make sure that the opposite sides are equally spaced from the center). Within this marked area, mark a second rectangle; this should be an even ½ inch in from the first. This marks the outside edge of the outer border.

5 Leave an even gap on all sides of 4¾ inches, then draw another border rectangle (66½ x 68 inches). This marks

the division between the inner and outer borders.

6 Leave an even gap of 4¼ inches on all sides and then draw the inner edge of the inner border – a rectangle measuring 58 x 59½ inches.

7 The pattern of the original quilt has a somewhat random air, although an attempt has been made to impose

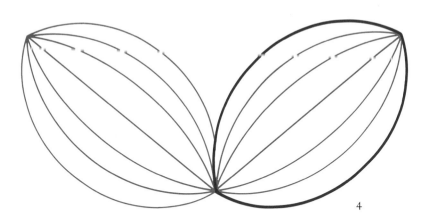

4

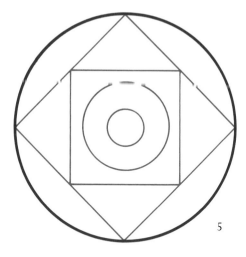

5

symmetry. There is no reason why you should not rearrange the design if you choose, and the easiest way to do this, or to repeat the original pattern, is to use photocopies. Scale up the templates and make cardboard templates in the usual way, then take each template and draw around it several times, filling a sheet of 8 x 10 paper.

8 Take photocopies of the templates; you will need about 56 copies of template 1, 8 of 2, 100 of 3, 50 of 4, 6 of 5, 28 of 6, 6 of 7, 24 of 8, 4 of 9, and 8 of template 10 (this allows some spares of shapes that are repeated frequently, so that you can alter the pattern, if you choose).

9 Set the photocopies aside, and start by drawing the central motif. The star-like outer shaping is the same as that of template 7, but expanded to measure 17 inches from point to point. The central two circles are the same as those of template 7, but enclosed within a square, which in turn is enclosed within a circle.

10 Next, cut out the photocopied shapes and pin them to the fabric top, filling the two borders and surrounding the marked central design. Either arrange the shapes as shown here, with the quarters of the design mirror-imaging each other, or make your own arrangement. Remember not to leave large gaps between shapes, as the batting will tend to move in large unquilted areas.

11 When you are happy with the arrangement of the shapes, use the templates to mark the design on the top.

QUILTING
12 Assemble the three layers – backing, batting, and the marked top (see page 17).

13 Quilt all marked lines, including the outer marked line.

14 When you have finished quilting, trim the batting back to within a scant ¾ inch of the outer quilted line.

15 Trim the top and backing fabrics to within ½ inch of the batting, then bring the top fabric over the edge of the batting, and turn in the edge of the backing fabric to meet it. Pin and baste.

16 Topstitch the front and back pieces neatly together, stitching close to the folded edges.

10

7

6

9

8

Templates

The following pages contain alternative templates for the small projects on pages 22-25 (see below), patchwork templates for the Pink Star project and alternative traditional quilting designs.

Counterclockwise from top right: lover's knot, concentric hearts, Devon quilt heart and scallop shell templates.

*ABOVE   Bisected patchwork templates
— see the pink and white star project
on page 77.*

ABOVE Create your own designs by using some of these traditional quilting running patterns.

Index

Acknowledgements

*With special thanks to Roderick James, Architect, Carpenter, Oak & Woodland Co. ltd,
Hall Farm, Thickwood Lane, Colerne, Chippenham, Wiltshire SN14 8BE.*

*Also to Robert and Josyane Young (Robert Young Antiques, 68 Battersea Bridge Road,
London SW11) and to Isobel Bird, all of whom opened their homes to let us
photograph there. Many thanks also to Katrin Cargill for styling the photographs, and
to Judy Greenwood and Trisha Jameson for their lovely quilts.*